THE SUBWAY CHRONICLES

*This book is dedicated to
the city of New York.*

I0050027

THE SUBWAY

catch the
MOST WANTED
Goosebumps® villains
UNDEAD OR ALIVE!

SCHOLASTIC, GOOSEBUMPS and associated logos
are trademarks and/or registered trademarks
of Scholastic Inc. All rights reserved.

SCHOLASTIC
scholastic.com/goosebumps

Available in print
and eBook editions

THE SCARIEST PLACE ON EARTH!

Goosebumps HorrorLand
HELP! WE HAVE STRANGE POWERS!
R.L. STINE
SCHOLASTIC

Goosebumps HorrorLand
ESCAPE FROM HORRORLAND
R.L. STINE
SCHOLASTIC

Goosebumps HorrorLand
THE STREETS OF PANIC PARK
R.L. STINE
SCHOLASTIC

Goosebumps HorrorLand
WHEN THE GHOST DOG HOWLS
R.L. STINE
SCHOLASTIC

Goosebumps HorrorLand
LITTLE SHOP OF HAMSTERS
R.L. STINE
SCHOLASTIC

Goosebumps HorrorLand
HEADS, YOU LOSE!
R.L. STINE
SCHOLASTIC

Goosebumps HorrorLand
WEIRDO HALLOWEEN
R.L. STINE
SCHOLASTIC

Goosebumps HorrorLand
THE WIZARD OF OOZE
R.L. STINE
SCHOLASTIC

HALL OF HORRORS—HALL OF FAME FOR THE TRULY TERRIFYING!

Goosebumps HorrorLand
SLAPPY NEW YEAR!
R.L. STINE
SCHOLASTIC

Goosebumps HorrorLand
THE HORROR AT CHILLER HOUSE
R.L. STINE
SCHOLASTIC

Goosebumps Hall of Horrors
CLAWS!
R.L. STINE
SCHOLASTIC

Goosebumps Hall of Horrors
NIGHT OF THE GIANT EVERYTHING
R.L. STINE
SCHOLASTIC

SCHOLASTIC

SCHOLASTIC and associated logos
are trademarks and/or registered
trademarks of Scholastic Inc.

www.scholastic.com/goosebumps

GBHL19H2

CHRONICLES

Scenes from Life in New York

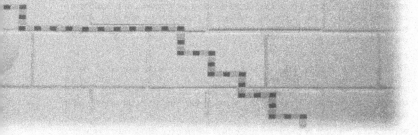

EDITED BY JACQUELIN CANGRO

℗ A PLUME BOOK

PLUME
Published by Penguin Group
Penguin Group (USA) Inc., 375 Hudson Street, New York, New York 10014, U.S.A. •
Penguin Group (Canada), 90 Eglinton Avenue East, Suite 700, Toronto, Ontario,
Canada M4P 2Y3 (a division of Pearson Penguin Canada Inc.) • Penguin Books
Ltd., 80 Strand, London WC2R 0RL, England • Penguin Ireland, 25 St. Stephen's Green,
Dublin 2, Ireland (a division of Penguin Books Ltd.) • Penguin Group (Australia),
250 Camberwell Road, Camberwell, Victoria 3124, Australia (a division of Pearson
Australia Group Pty. Ltd.) • Penguin Books India Pvt. Ltd., 11 Community Centre,
Panchsheel Park, New Delhi – 110 017, India • Penguin Books (NZ), cnr Airborne
and Rosedale Roads, Albany, Auckland 1310, New Zealand (a division of Pearson
New Zealand Ltd.) • Penguin Books (South Africa) (Pty.) Ltd., 24 Sturdee Avenue,
Rosebank, Johannesburg 2196, South Africa

Penguin Books Ltd., Registered Offices: 80 Strand, London WC2R 0RL, England

First published by Plume, a member of Penguin Group (USA) Inc.

10 9 8 7 6 5 4 3 2

Copyright © Jacquelin Cangro, 2006
All rights reserved

Pages 211–212 constitute an extension of the copyright page.

℗ REGISTERED TRADEMARK—MARCA REGISTRADA

LIBRARY OF CONGRESS CATALOGING-IN-PUBLICATION DATA
The subway chronicles : scenes from life in New York / edited by Jacquelin Cangro.
    p. cm.
  ISBN 0-452-28779-0 (trade pbk.)
  1. Subways—New York (State)—New York—Fiction.   2. New York (N.Y.)—Social
life and customs—Fiction.   3. Short stories, American.   I. Cangro, Jacquelin.
PS648. S5S79 2006
813'.6—dc22   2006010953

Set in Minion and Trajan
Designed by Eve L. Kirch

Without limiting the rights under copyright reserved above, no part of this publication
may be reproduced, stored in or introduced into a retrieval system, or transmitted, in
any form, or by any means (electronic, mechanical, photocopying, recording, or otherwise), without the prior written permission of both the copyright owner and the above
publisher of this book.

PUBLISHER'S NOTE
The scanning, uploading, and distribution of this book via the Internet or via any
other means without the permission of the publisher is illegal and punishable by law.
Please purchase only authorized electronic editions, and do not participate in or encourage electronic piracy of copyrighted materials. Your support of the author's rights
is appreciated.

BOOKS ARE AVAILABLE AT QUANTITY DISCOUNTS WHEN USED TO PROMOTE PRODUCTS
OR SERVICES. FOR INFORMATION PLEASE WRITE TO PREMIUM MARKETING DIVISION,
PENGUIN GROUP (USA) INC., 375 HUDSON STREET, NEW YORK, NEW YORK 10014.

CONTENTS

INTRODUCTION

W hile watching a blizzard from her window, Eudora Welty
saw an old woman trudge through the driving snow. What
could make her go outside under such terrible conditions? Welty
wondered. Her imagined answers turned into the acclaimed short
story, "A Worn Path."

The subway is my window, and I suspect, the window of many
writers in this anthology. Whether I'm writing about a hurricane in
Florida or a World War II army sergeant, my pages are filled with
gestures and conversation picked up from riders on the subway. (To
the lady next to me who blew continuous bubbles with a wad of
purple gum from the Village to Coney Island: You're next.) Truth be
told, I am writing this while riding the F train. It seems appropriate,
but it's not unusual. I do most of my writing on the subway. You
might think it's too distracting: beggars asking for change, sticky
floors and seats, the smell of fried chicken. But I can't imagine more
fertile ground for a writer. Many writers may get inspiration tool-
ing around in the insular worlds of their cars, but I'm glad I don't
have to be worried about when the muse will strike next. I have an
ever-changing cast of characters every time the train doors open.
And so do the writers on the pages that follow. Lawrence Block, in

"Collecting Old Subway Cars," concurs: "Writers who don't take the subway? They must be out of their minds."

There's probably no better character to find on the subway than your look-alike, a person who resembles you so closely that even your friends are fooled. That's exactly who Robert Lanham finds on the L train in "Straphanger Doppelgänger." Francine Prose's encounter with a pervert in "A Breakup Story" solidifies her career choice. But it's not always the strangers on the subway who give us pause. It can be those closest to us. In "Transfer," Leigh Stolle discovers the tenacity and affection of her elderly Midwestern parents, and Johnny Temple's friend gets a reality check of biblical proportions in "The First Annual Three-Borough Subway Party." Sometimes the subway itself is the most interesting character. Stan Fischler recalls the thrill of his hair blowing in the breeze on an elevated train trip to Coney Island when he was four years old. Boris Fishman compares the beauty and functionality of the New York City and Moscow subway systems, and Ken Wheaton gets back to business-as-usual after the London bombings.

There are two euphemisms most often used when referring to the subway. One is that it is the lifeblood of New York City. The facts and figures don't lie. Every day five million people wait on one of 468 station platforms to ride one or more of twenty-seven subway lines. The other euphemism is that the New York subway is a microcosm of world culture. The train is the great equalizer. When the doors close, all of us—black or white, Sephardic or Catholic, Chinese or Indian—are going together, and no one will arrive any faster or in better style. The essays in this anthology take those euphemisms and dig deeper because when you get down to it, the subway is about the people and their stories. In fact, the idea for this collection began as a Thanksgiving dinner conversation, with each person trying to outdo the other's best subway story. That's why whether you ride the subway every day or have never stepped foot underground, I bet you will find common threads of love, fear, anger, worry, exhilaration, and comradeship among these essays.

I invite you to turn the page, stand clear of the closing doors, and join us. We're making all local stops.

—Jacquelin Cangro

THE SUBWAY CHRONICLES

OPENING DAY

Tim McLoughlin

The weather was perfect this year on June twenty-first as I rode the N train to Keyspan Park for the fifth opening-day home game of the Brooklyn Cyclones. I am one of those New Yorkers who chronically laments the Disnifying of the city—particularly Times Square and Coney Island—but hasn't missed an opening day yet. I like to think of myself as part of the problem.

The renovation of the Coney Island station is finally complete, and you can ride directly to the shore once again. It's an odd, retro-modern looking stop now, like something out of a Jetsons cartoon, or the old TWA terminal at JFK. Forty years ago it would have been the coolest space imaginable. Now it looks instantly archaic, like modern Soviet architecture. There's nothing worse than old cool.

Plus they destroyed all the shops that had inhabited the station. The Terminal Bar and Phillip's Candies were my favorites. The bar had been closed for years, but the candy shop remained open for business right up until the station began its renovation. It had been there since 1907, and I remember the day that my friend Andy discovered his grandfather in a photograph of customers, taped to the store window, that was dated 1930.

I had set off for the game directly from my job, so I had taken the R at Borough Hall and switched to the N at DeKalb Avenue. I was on the express for about twenty seconds when the announcement sounded over the public address system: *Passenger Timmy McLoughlin, please report to the motorman's booth.*

It was Kenny Garguilo. We first met more than twenty years ago when we both worked in the textbook department at the main branch of Barnes & Noble; and being a couple of white ethnic outer-borough kids with little regard for higher education and no predilection for crime, we chased each other through the Civil Service system for a couple of decades. Kenny had been a 911 operator, then a cop, before becoming a motorman. I was a night watchman for the Transit Authority before becoming a court officer, then a court clerk. I run into Kenny once or twice a year, either on the subway or at Nathan's in Coney Island on his meal break.

I looked for the motorman's booth—as instructed—receiving questioning glances from fellow straphangers as I made my way through the cars. I could see people wondering if I was really important or just a terrorist. Kenny and I caught up on old times and traded war stories for a while, then I left him alone to chauffeur me the rest of the way to the stadium.

Talking to Kenny brought my Transit Authority days back in a rush. I've always had the love/hate relationship with the system that one feels for the company in a company town. My father and two uncles were career transit workers. My uncle Mike was a bus driver, and uncle Charlie was a mechanic, working on subway motors and undercarriages. My father was a boiler maintainer, heating the enormous repair shops called "car barns" in Coney Island, East New York, and 207th Street in Manhattan.

My own very brief career was, as I said, that of a night watchman. Of course, since garbage collectors are sanitation engineers, and meter maids are traffic-enforcement agents, my title could not officially be Night Watchman. I was a Property Protection Agent. Really. On my first day I was issued a blue hat that looked vaguely police-ish and a little yellow plastic flashlight, and I was assigned the midnight to eight a.m. shift in the Coney Island yards, there to ensure, in the mid-1980s, that no one would place any graffiti on the thousand or so subway cars that were housed in my area of the seventy-five-acre yard. In a very small way, I understood the frustration of a border patrol officer with two hundred miles to monitor and nine hours of darkness to contend with. It was a job defined by acceptable levels of failure.

Every night I would relieve the four-to-twelve man, sign in, and begin my clockwinds, which involved carrying a large, heavy, ancient clock sheathed in leather and outfitted with a shoulder strap, around the train yard once every hour. At five or six locations along the fence line, there were small metal containers, about the size of ashtrays in a car. Each container held a key secured by a chain. The key was to be inserted into a slot in the back of the clock and turned, causing an indentation in the tape that spooled its way through the innards of the gizmo, thus recording that you were where you were supposed to be, when you were supposed to be there. Sturdy as the clocks were, most of the watchmen figured out how to disable them pretty quickly and often spent the night sitting in the little phone booth–like shacks on the periphery of the yards. In East New York you learned to unscrew the lightbulb so that no one shot at you. In the morning the trains were covered in graffiti, you filled out a report, and went home. It was a full life.

On the rare occasion when I did encounter a graffiti artist—or vandal, as my profession mandated I regard them—I would chase them away rather than detain them. With absolutely no training, no police or peace officer status, and only the aforementioned yellow flashlight for equipment, I did not see my job exactly in a law enforcement context. I felt more like the ranger in Jellystone Park, ever vigilant to prevent Yogi Bear from snatching picnic baskets. I think the graffiti kids felt the same way. They always gave me the courtesy of running away when I confronted them, even if they were in a group. I came to recognize some of the regulars, and they would casually acknowledge me outside the train yard if I walked over to Spumoni Garden for my meal break. I generally considered them harmless, but was once rocked from my idyll when they torched a stolen car across the street from the yard, about thirty feet from my booth. It was two thirty in the morning, and I'd been on the phone with a friend who worked the night shift in a brokerage house on Wall Street. I was sitting with my back to the street and first saw the flames reflected in the glass of the booth. That resulted in the one and only 911 call of my career.

If I did not get to know the muralists up close, I made up for it by studying my coworkers intensely. They were in many ways more tribal than the graffiti kids. Every train yard has its own ethnic vibe, and Coney Island's was distinctly Italian. Small but elaborate gardens were planted anywhere there was a bare patch of earth, and rows of tomato plants were staked between the tracks. Although the number of running trains is cut down dramatically at night, since the system never shuts down, repair and maintenance work goes on 24/7.

I worked in several yards by the end of that summer. As the new man, I was assigned vacation-relief, which meant that I moved around the city, filling in a week here and there as people took time off. I'd cut through the barns on my winds, or on breaks, and watch the work crews—called gangs—roam the floor, then pounce on a subway car as though it was a wounded critter cut from the herd. Six to eight men would jump into the pit below the car and yank more machinery from the undercarriage than would be expected on the space shuttle. In three or four hours it was all replaced, and they would move to another car and begin again.

During the day each yard was as bustling and self-contained as a small town, but even at night there was a good level of activity. I'd grown up in and around the yards, and what strikes me as unusual about it now, is that then it did not strike me as an unusual place at all.

The barns are huge and built like airplane hangars. There might be more than a thousand men working at peak hours. Just men, by the way. During my stint, the train yards, car barns, and machine shops were an entirely masculine domain. The whole compound resembled an army base as much as a village.

Although my job was generally considered to be preventing theft or damage to property from outside sources, we were also supposed to watch for infractions of rules by employees. Since one of the rules was that no unauthorized persons were permitted in the yards, and since I'd spent the night sleeping on a cot in the boiler room of most of those yards in the summertime when I was a kid, I kind of took that rule as more of a suggestion.

When I worked there, anything and everything was for sale. In Coney Island I could buy condoms or prayer cards from various entrepreneurs operating out of their lockers. At 207th Street there was a corner of the barn known as Mulberry Street, where on Fridays, all the clothing and merchandise was displayed.

At the Thirty-ninth Street yard, which was relatively small and always smelled of diesel fuel because it housed work trains, the signal maintainers kept dogs. There were five of them, and on the few occasions I was sent there, they patiently waited for me outside my booth and walked with me as I made my winds.

A dozen or more of the men lived in each yard; their numbers shifting as people got divorced, got evicted, or just became crazy. The ones who became crazy stayed the longest, and I remember one who cried when his foreman told him he had to leave because he had retired.

There were odd, makeshift living spaces rigged in closets and small rooms. At 207th Street I saw two men living in the motor room above the freight elevator, sleeping on rollaway beds on opposite sides of the enormous, loud engine. They all bathed in homemade showers, did laundry in concrete garage sinks, and dried their clothing by draping it over subway cars they were repairing. Though no one had shown me a written rule stating that employees were not permitted to reside at their work site, I was pretty sure it was not what the city government had in mind.

Workers cooked on the many stoves and refrigerators in the numerous barns—also prohibited—and at the two full kitchens cobbled together in Coney Island, and the three in upper Manhattan. To their credit, the guys at 207th Street painted the refrigerators to blend in with the walls or hid them in the rear of the small workshops. Some men prepared elaborate breakfasts and lunches and sold them to coworkers, operating little businesses on the side. I felt rather like Claude Rains in *Casablanca* when, years after my departure, I read that a surprise inspection had revealed more than one hundred refrigerators and stoves at the upper Manhattan Barn. A photo showed them piled in a heap in the parking lot. I was shocked, shocked, to discover the contraband had been on the premises.

What was most surprising about all of the eccentricity I encountered was its one solid tie to unwavering logic. From the pack rats of Coney Island, filling entire storage rooms with their scavenged treasures to the mountain men of 207th Street, carrying hunting bows across Broadway to unload a few quivers into paper targets propped against mountains of salt in the unmanned Sanitation Department warehouse, everyone adhered to the golden rule. Their term for it was "making service," and it was remarkably simple: The trains had to run. Whatever else happened, you had to make service. And they did. I think that they all understood—from the conscientious to the shiftless to the just plain nuts—that the reason their fringe society could exist in the middle of New York City as it did was that things ran smoothly. When things do not run smoothly, management sticks in its ugly proboscis. And as any blue-collar worker can attest, management's idea of solving a problem is throwing all your refrigerators away and declaring the problem solved, usually without knowing what the problem is.

So the trains ran, and continue to run, I noted, as we slowed to a lazy stop in the newly renovated Coney Island station. As part of the Transit Authority's recent efforts to distract public attention from mounting fare increases and its own very private books, it ballyhoos advances in modernization, cost cutting, and public service. Don't believe the hype. The trains always ran, and the trains will always run, largely because of strange guys with wrenches and welding torches and grinding wheels. Guys who brainstorm to invent tools to fix problems not foreseen by the manufacturers of the equipment they maintain, and then create those tools on the spot in the blacksmith shop. Guys whose bosses will keep throwing out refrigerators to show *their* bosses that they can solve problems. And their bosses will keep trying to flense the workplace of fun and eccentricity until it is as sanitized and bland as the new Coney Island station. And they'll fail. At least they have, I'm pleased to say, for the past two generations.

By the way, the Cyclones won that night 10–7. Fifth straight opening day win, and against the hated Staten Island Yankees no less. There's nothing like enjoying a hot dog and a cold beer while watching a ball game and a Coney Island sunset. Of course there's also Neil Diamond's video image exhorting you to join him in singing "Sweet Caroline" during the seventh inning stretch, and way too many chintzy advertising plugs but, as I've established, I'm part of the problem.

I dozed briefly on the N during the ride home and awakened startled and momentarily disoriented. I checked my feet instinctively, always remembering my father's admonition that if you fell asleep on the subway someone would steal your shoes. But I was having a good day. They were still there.

Tim McLoughlin's *debut novel,* Heart of the Old Country, *was a selection of the Barnes & Noble Discover Great New Writers program and has been optioned for a film. He is the editor of the* Brooklyn Noir *anthology series, and his short fiction has been included in the* Best American Mystery Stories 2005.

A BREAKUP STORY

Francine Prose

It was the summer of 1966. I was living at home, with my parents, in Brooklyn. That July, Richard Speck had murdered eight student nurses in Chicago. Their innocent faces, tilted at that cheerful graduation-photo angle as if they were gazing into a bright future that happened to be located just beyond the edge of the shot, stared at me from the front page of every newspaper. And I understood that they had found their darker future waiting for them on a hot summer night in a townhouse in South Chicago.

I thought about that crime a lot. I wondered what my friends and I would have done had there been eight of us and one of him. I thought about *every* crime a lot. I was nineteen, and romantic, and I believed in my heart that I was destined to die a horrible death at the hands of some demented mass murderer. At the time, that eventuality seemed much more likely than the absurd possibility that I would live to be the age I am now.

It was the summer between my sophomore and and junior year of college. It was, it seems to me now, the cusp between my being a girl who, despite a healthy dose of rebelliousness, did mostly what my parents wanted—that is, what they considered important: school, boys, my future. My college boyfriend was in California, and I was dating a friend of his in a sort of halfhearted and entirely platonic way—halfhearted and platonic partly because I found him nice enough but not attractive, and partly because he (with medical school already gleaming in *his* bright future) was exactly the sort of boy my parents would have liked me to marry.

I was going to summer school at Columbia University, taking a course in writing (I wanted to be a writer, but no one else in my family approved, and I myself secretly hoped that I would think of something easier and more ordinary and less scary) and another course in architecture (which I secretly hoped would be that easy, ordinary, and unscary thing). I hated my architecture course and loved the writing seminar, which was taught by a guy who had a complete, endearing, and in fact sort of charismatic lack of interest in our writing. Rather than read it, or be burdened with it in any way, he spent the entire class telling stories about his beatnik past, his years at Black Mountain College, and his friendship with literary bad boys like William Burroughs and Hubert Selby Jr. Nothing could have made me happier.

So perhaps the reason I so fully expected to be murdered by some psycho killer was that I knew that it would spare me from having to make some hard decisions that, I was beginning to sense, I would soon be called upon to make.

Every day I took the subway from the Newkirk Avenue station in Brooklyn to 116th and Broadway and back again. It was a long ride, well over an hour in each direction, but somehow it seemed like nothing. For one thing, I was used to long commutes. Every day, from the fifth grade until the day I graduated from high school, I took the train from my home in Flatbush to downtown Brooklyn, where I went to school. On weekends, my friends and I went into the city to hang out. There was nothing to do in Brooklyn, not then, and if you wanted to have any fun at all, it meant taking the train into Manhattan.

We made it as enjoyable as we could. In high school, we always rode in the first car with our faces pressed against the front window, watching the light show streaming at us as we rushed through the black tunnel. My friends and I lived at different stops, though mostly on the same line, so we knew that the first car was where we would find one another if we happened to be on the same train, which we were more often than one would have expected.

I'd grown up on the subway—I loved the subway, I'd always loved the subway, and I still do. But that summer, something was off, something was wrong. Each time I left home, I was anxious in a way I'd never been before. Perhaps it was the murder of the nurses. Perhaps I'd been away from home too long, off at college, and had lost the ease with which I'd always swam, like a fish, in what had always seemed to me the friendly, welcoming waters of New York.

At moments, for no apparent reason, my heart would begin to race. I suppose I was having controllable, mini-versions of what we now call panic attacks. And also for no good reason, my new fears collected around Times Square, the 42nd Street station, through which I had to weave a fairly complex course as I changed from the Seventh Avenue line that went up the Upper West Side to what was then called the BMT, which took me to and from Brooklyn.

Much has been written about the "old" Times Square, before it got cleaned up and Disnified. In fact, there's still something great about it; after all this time, driving downtown through Times Square at night never fails to deliver the paradoxically reliable thrill. But it's true, it *was* better then: a true paradise of porn palaces and pimps, street hustlers and dope dealers, all of it seedier, more mysterious, more glamorous and dangerous than it is today. It was more exciting in every way. More . . . subterranean. And the 42nd Street subway station was where the subterranean actually went underground.

My friends and I were repeatedly warned by our parents not to go to the Times Square station, not to walk through there if we could help it and, under no circumstances, to hang out there. Of course, it was our favorite place to hang out. We loved the smell of dampness and hot dogs, the crowds, the people who seemed to have nothing to do but stand around looking sinister, the music blaring out of Times Square Records, where we went to pore through bins of old 45s, looking for 1950s classics.

And yet that summer I found myself having those shaky, short-of-breath moments each time I had to walk through the twisting corridors that connected one subway line with another. I felt that something was waiting for me, just as something had been waiting for those student nurses in Chicago. I held my breath and rushed through the tunnels, and not until I was on the train could I exhale and begin to breathe again.

To ride the subway every day is to be reminded on a daily basis what animals we are, what we have in common with those species with whom we share parallel rungs on the evolutionary ladder. We operate on instinct; we learn better than to make the eye contact that might violate some unspoken code, and so use our antennae, our radar finely attuned to the slightest disturbance in the field: something out of place, something unusual, someone standing too close or looking at us just a little too long. Growing up in New York, you grow up with that radar; it's not anything you have to learn or develop. It's just there.

It was late July or early August. I still had a month or so of summer school to get through, and then a little longer before I would head off to college again. It was a weekday afternoon. I was finished with school and headed downtown from Columbia.

I was going home to work on a story that was due in my writing class. It seems likely to me now that someone had noticed that not a word of student writing had been discussed all summer; someone had spoken to our teacher. And suddenly we had a week in which to write a story.

I was writing a truly terrible story about a romantic breakup. And that was what I was thinking about as I entered the tunnels beneath

Times Square. For a weekday afternoon it was strangely deserted, but the subways were less crowded then, and it was a season when many New Yorkers are out of town and the tourists know better than to brave the late-summer heat.

I was alone in the tunnel, halfway through. Once more I began to get that strange, slightly breathless, slightly intoxicated feeling. And that was when I saw him coming toward me.

He looked, it seems to me now, like a sex pervert from Central Casting: short, fat, greasy, shiny business suit, pencil mustache, the works. He was carrying a little briefcase as if he were rushing to an appointment, but the minute he and I saw each other, it was clear that his appointment was with me. I suppose I could have turned and run. But I kept thinking that I was being paranoid, that anything sinister was all in my imagination—that my instincts were wrong, my antenna quivering over nothing. Really, he was just a seedy little guy on his way back from lunch. And something in me rebelled. Who the hell was he, anyway? Didn't I have as much right to walk through the tunnel as he did? And yet the fact was, he was eyeing me, moving in a peculiar way, stooping, then walking again. Later when I saw sick animals in the zoo, something in the weave of their walk would always remind me of him.

We approached each other, and now I knew that something was going to happen. And then it did. At the moment as we passed one another, his hand shot out like some fork or tendril or tentacle. He grabbed my breast. He grabbed it hard, and squeezed.

Astonishing both of us, I stopped in my tracks, the proverbial deer in the headlights. We stared at each other. And we stood like that, for a few seconds, me standing there, him grabbing my breast, until the spell broke, and I gasped and ran away as he scurried off in the opposite direction.

My first instinct was to tell someone, report him, tell the police. As soon as I emerged from the corridor, I saw a tall young man in a blue uniform.

"Officer," I said, "listen, there was this man, he grabbed me, he—"

"I'd love to help you," said the young man, who I now realized was not a young man at all but just a kid, "but I'm only an Eagle Scout."

Already the adrenaline was leaving me, weak-kneed and shaky but solid on my feet. And somehow it all began to seem funny. I laughed, and kept on laughing as I made my way to the train. But I kept on looking over my shoulder. I couldn't stop thinking that, despite the furtive rodentlike haste with which he'd run away, he'd returned and was following me.

I went home and started working on my story, but the romantic breakup story no longer held the slightest interest.

For the rest of that summer, I expected to see him every time I walked through the station. After a while I got so nervous that, when I changed trains, I went upstairs and walked down Forty-second Street and then went back down into the station. It meant paying a whole extra fare—which at that time was only fifteen cents—but I didn't care; I would have done anything to avoid that underground corridor. I thought about the pervert breast-grabber as much as I'd thought about Richard Speck and the nurses. It was as if we had a *relationship*. And eventually, as my memory of the event began to dim, I came to feel as if I had imagined him, made him up, conjured him into appearing.

I began to wonder about him, about who he was, about what pressures in his life had pushed him to the point of grabbing strange women's breasts in subway tunnels. In that way, he stopped being a guy who had groped me, and became a fictional character.

I threw away the breakup story I'd been working on, and I put my pervert into a story. I wrote it in one night—in fact, the night before our stories were due. I'm fairly sure that the pervert story was equally as terrible as the breakup story. But, as I should have expected, given what I knew of his literary tastes, my teacher seemed to like it. I got an A in my writing class and a D in architecture.

I no longer have the story, nor can I remember what exactly it was like. But I do have the memory of that summer, of that encounter in the subway station, and of the way that corridor beneath

Times Square turned out to be part of the path that led to my becoming a writer.

Francine Prose's most recent books are A Changed Man, *a novel, and* Caravaggio: Painter of Miracles, *which is part of the Eminent Lives series. Her novel* Blue Angel *was a finalist for the National Book Award.* Reading Like a Writer, *a book about learning to write by reading literature, will appear from HarperCollins in fall 2006. She is a contributing editor at* Harper's *and writes frequently for numerous other publications.*

PORNO MAN AND I VERSUS THE FEMINIST AVENGER AND DISPLACED ANGER MAN

Daniels Parseliti

A long the N line in Astoria, Queens, only one stop separates 30th Avenue from Ditmars Boulevard. It's a stretch of track that I've ridden many times, seeing as it's the commute from my house to my girlfriend's.

The train rolled in and I sat down next to two not-unattractive hipster girls who were chatting about something boring. They sat to my right and gave me that gentrification-in-progress feeling that has been sweeping the neighborhood since I first moved to Astoria four and a half years ago. I sat there for a couple of seconds, thinking about the demographic shift in the neighborhood, thinking about how, in fact, I was part of that shift, and what to my wandering eye did appear but a homeless man flashing me a picture of two gigantic breasts in a porno magazine. *Ahhh,* I thought. *Not total homogenization.* The hipster girls had looked too. "Oh my God," whispered one to the other. She turned away from the picture and placed her right hand over her right eye, apparently with the intention of shielding the periphery of her vision from contamination by any porno light that might reflect off the magazine.

Porno Man was in his late fifties, maybe early sixties. He was sitting on the opposite side of the car, about five or six people down to my right. I think he originally caught my attention by waving the magazine and saying, "Look at this one, eh!" Sitting down and being immediately presented with a picture of two huge naked breasts made me laugh. Maybe not really laugh, but I let out a big puff of air that made my lips vibrate in a kind of loud, loose raspberry sound. Or maybe I sounded more like a horse. Anyway, Porno Man followed suit, laughing and taking my noise as an endorsement of his behavior. "It's good, it's good, no?" The entire train looked at me, and then at him, and then at me again. I don't think I have ever been the impetus for so many a head turn. *All right,* I thought to myself, *I just made a loud noise on a somewhat crowded train, and that noise has linked me to this guy who is flashing pictures of naked women to the general public.* I had scoundrelized myself in the eyes of the passengers. I had become *That Guy,* that guy who indulges the other guy who shouldn't be indulged. I put my head down and chuckled a little more; I couldn't help thinking that the situation was quite funny, and on the whole rather harmless. If these people were mad at me for unintentionally supporting a guy who wanted to flash porn around on the train, then damn the porno, let them be mad.

Porno Man was obviously not in good mental health, but he seemed content with flashing pictures of boobs and crotches to the passengers. I didn't think that he was going to take his routine, if you could call it that, any further. He was what I had always imagined a dirty old man to be, and I had always imagined dirty old men as somewhat harmless as long as no children were around. This said, I'd be lying if I didn't tell you that the question, "What would Judith Butler do?" careened off one of the norms made explicit by the situation. Moreover, what was going on in Porno Man's head to make him think that flashing porn around on the train was a good idea?

Well, Porno Man kept trying to get my attention all throughout the five-minute ride: "Pop-pee, ey ey Pop-pee! Look at this one! This is a good one, no?!" he would say and hold up a new picture, first to me, then he would give it a nice slow pan so that everyone on the train who made the mistake of looking at him would get an eye-ful of porn. He also made several gruntish noises like, "Ohh yeah! Ohh yeah!" nodding his head and smiling with approval as he flipped the pages of his magazine to find the commuters another treat. It was becoming obvious to me that my little vibrating lip laugh *had* egged him on, and now he was getting really excited (not sexually excited, at least from what I observed. It seemed more like kid-showing-off-his-new-toys excited).

The train was about to pull into the Ditmars station, the final stop. The door at the opposite end of the train opens and in comes one of the regulars. Now, by regulars I mean one of the people who generally works the N or W train for donations. This woman looked healthier than she used to, and I fished in my pocket for change to give her. She was standing in the middle of the train, giving her usual speech, when Porno Man decided to grace her with his porno presence.

"Hey hey," he yelled, and held up a picture bearing some kind of explicit content.

"Oh, that is fucking disgusting!" she screamed. And when I say screamed, I mean *loud*.

And so began the escalation.

"Put that shit away, put that fucking shit away, you sick fuck! There are women on this train, don't you have any respect for women?!" She was screaming. Porno Man didn't seem to care what she thought; he just wanted to show off his porn. Not content with screaming, the regular runs over to Porno Man and grabs the mag-azine. Things are getting more than a bit tense. "There are fucking women on this train, you asshole. That makes me so mad. Don't you respect women?"

Porno Man and the regular—let's call her the Feminist Avenger—

were now engaged in a loud tug-of-war over the magazine. "Is *that* what Judith Butler would do?" I asked myself.

Porno Man would not let go. The Feminist Avenger reared back and began to slap Porno Man as hard as she could. Not a gentle "Sir, I demand satisfaction!" slap that comes from the elbow and wrist, but a barrage of fully wound-up at the waist, open-fist punches that resonated off Porno Man's rapidly reddening face. He finally let go of the magazine and put both of his hands in front of his face to try to lessen the impact.

At first it appeared that the medium-size man in leather jacket and bandana who had entered the scene from my left was going to break up the Porno Man/Feminist Avenger bout. No such luck for Porno Man. Let's call this new guy Displaced Anger Man. While the Feminist Avenger was busy whaling on Porno Man's face with her open hand, Displaced Anger Man saw fit to grab Porno Man by the forehead and *slam* the back of his skull into the train wall. His head went *thwap* into the aluminum, and his baseball cap took on an awkward, half-on-half-off tilt. Porno Man, looking visibly shaken, straightened his head, only to have it *thwap*ed again against the aluminum, this time harder than the first. The force of the blow knocked Porno Man's hat off, and Displaced Anger Man leaned forward with all his weight, grinding Porno Man's skull between his palm and the aluminum.

We weren't in funny Porno Man Land anymore. Everyone on the train had just entered Witness to Assault Land. And the gravity in Witness to Assault Land is much stronger than the gravity in Porno Man Land. I started to feel cold. That coldness migrated from my flesh inward, to the muscles of my neck, tightening them noticeably. Throughout the car, the cold gravity asserted its force on everyone. Anyone who had been talking stopped.

Displaced Anger Man now held the porno magazine in his right hand. Standing over a quivering Porno Man, Displaced Anger Man slapped him in the face, as hard as he could, with the porno magazine. Now came the really strange part. Displaced Anger Man yelled at Porno Man, "What's wrong with you, huh? Don't you respect women? Haven't you got respect for women?" Porno Man groaned a little, then was whaled again with the magazine. The questions continued: "There are women on this train. Don't you respect women? You got no respect for women?" The entrance of Displaced Anger Man, the head shove, and the porno smacking all took place in maybe fifteen or twenty seconds. During this time I had three distinct thoughts: *(1) Damn, this is strange. (2) I should really do something. (3) Does Displaced Anger Man really care about Porno Man's respect for women, and what on earth is his motivation?*

The train was finally in the station. The doors opened and the hipsters unhiply sprinted out the door, along with everyone else on the train except for me and the three quarrelers. I was still sitting down, watching what was happening, and I had another thought. It was very clear: *I can't let this guy keep getting hit. The guy hitting him doesn't look like he is going to stop anytime soon. In fact, he looks like he is enjoying it.*

One more time Porno Man was *thwaped* in the face with the magazine, and before I knew it, I was standing in front of Porno Man, face-to-face with Displaced Anger Man. He was older than I thought, some gray in his goatee, and a couple of inches shorter than me. He had a big flashlight in his jacket pocket, and I kept scanning his person for something that he might hit me with. He looked very confused. "You gotta stop," I said.

"What?" asked Displaced Anger Man.

"I said, you need to stop. Look, the guy is obviously fucked up, you can't just go hitting him like that." Behind me Porno Man groaned pathetically.

"What if that was your mother?" said Displaced Anger Man. I really couldn't believe what I was hearing. Not because it was logically impossible for this guy to have a grasp on gender inequality; assuming that I was feeling very charitable with my attributions of feminist stances at the time, maybe, just maybe, I could credit him with a very rough form of militant feminism. No, it's just that if this guy really was a militant feminist, I don't think he would have waited for the Feminist Avenger's explosion of anger to make his own position evident.

"I don't care who it is, my mother, your mother, you need to stop hitting him. End of story. Get off the train." I'm sure I was yelling and swearing, but it is hard to remember, what with my heart in my ears and all. I know I was screaming when I said, "Get off the train!"

The Feminist Avenger grabbed Displaced Anger Man's arm and started to pull him toward the open door. "Come on," she said. "Just chill out. Let's go." I watched them get off the train, and I got off as well, leaving slumped Porno Man the car's sole occupant.

Since then I've thought a lot about why I did what I did. Maybe I felt guilty because I laughed and somehow motivated Porno Man to pursue his public service porn announcements. Maybe that's why I got up and stood between him and Displaced Anger Man—because I felt in some capacity responsible for his actions. During the whole escalation I kept asking myself, *What does Displaced Anger Man have to do to Porno Man in order for me to intervene? Hit him really hard? Hit him enough times? Stab him? Take out a gun?* In the midst of firing off all of these questions to myself, I was struck by the fact that no one was doing anything.

There are myriad possible reasons for inaction. Action entails consequence and responsibility. Helping Porno Man required acknowledging, at least implicitly, that a homeless man feels pain, has beliefs, memory—in short, is a person who shares many things in common with everyone else. And acknowledging the fact of Porno Man's personhood opens up further problems, particularly, "Do I now need to help *every* homeless person I see in the city because I helped this one?" By ignoring Porno Man, the crowd on the train felt like they saved themselves from the problematic question. The only person who seemed demonstrably offended was *someone begging for money*, so the crowd could conclude that no one of consequence was involved, only the homeless and poor, easily ignored.

In many ways the above explanation makes sense to me. I can imagine why every passenger in the train car refused to act on the situation. In retrospect, I can imagine myself not acting. What I found at the time, however, was my mind asking that one question, *Should I do something?* over and over again. Then, suddenly, I was thinking, *I should; I should help.* I'm not sure what made me conclude that I should do something. There was no clear if a, then b; a therefore b. There was just a sequence of events and a vague transition from the question, *Should I do something?* to the assertion, *I should do something.*

It was at about this point, the point at which I decided that I should do something, that, as Wittgenstein would say, I hit bedrock. My spade turned and explanation gave way to practice. Because even if I could find some way to explain how I concluded that I should help Porno Man, there was nothing I could see that took me from the belief that I should help him to the actual action. It was simply as if something rose up, not in me, but under me, and pushed me between the two.

Daniels Parseliti *is a writer living in Queens, New York. He spends his time making fiction, philosophy, and pasta sauce, though only the sauce yields income. He has co-written a play that was produced twice in NYC and is currently working on a novel. Daniels can be reached at intuitconcept@hotmail.com.*

SUBWAY

Colson Whitehead

After those steps turnstiles spin and schemes kick in, where to stand and wait. It is hard to escape the suspicion that your train just left, the last squeal of your train drained away the moment you reached the platform, and if you had acted differently everything would be better. You should have left sooner, primped less. Reconsiderations: taking a cab, grabbing a bus, hoofing it. No, it's too far and the train is coming. It must be coming. Why else would you stand there.

This is the fabled journey underground, folks, and it's going to get a whole lot worse before it gets better. On the opposite track it's a field of greener grass, you gotta beat trains off with a stick. From his secret booth the announcer scares and reassures alternately. The postures on the platform sag or stiffen appropriately. With a dial controlling the amount of static. What are their rooms like, the men at the microphones. One day the fiscal improprieties of the subway announcer's union will be exposed and that will be the end of the hot tubs and lobster, but until then they break out the bubbly. Look down the tunnel one more time and your behavior will describe a psychiatric disorder. It's infectious. They take turns looking down into the darkness and the platform is a clock: the more people standing dumb, the more time has passed since the last train. The people fall from above into hourglass dunes. Collect like seconds.

There's a culture for platforms and a culture for between stations. On the platform there are strategies of where seats will appear when the doors open, of where you want to be when you get off, of how to outmaneuver these impromptu nemeses. So many variables, everyone's a mathematician with an advanced degree. Wait. Those elephantine ears of hers. Does she know something he doesn't, she's moving closer to the edge, and then he hears the roar, too. The herd trembles, the lion approaches, instincts awaken. The jaws slide apart and the people step inside. Various sounds of gorging.

Which car will you choose. Take your pick. In the happy-go-lucky car the wattage of their smiles brightens the tunnels. In the no-particular-place-to-go car they are recumbent. In the going-to-be-late car the grimace festival is in full swing. In the had-a-long-day car there are no seats. So again we must ask, which car will you choose. Dilemmas escalate. Can I make it to the seat before she gets there. Their eyes meet and they calculate distance. Stared down once again he gives up, such is his lot, and he leans against the conductor's door. At the next station the conductor has to shove against to get out.

Let 'em out, let 'em out. From stop to stop oblong advertisements suddenly get interesting in a strange sort of way. Along the fungi hall of fame we are introduced to ailments. Has anybody ever in history copied down the phone number of the dermatologist with the sinister name. After all these years he still hopes the needy will receive his revolutionary technique but for now must make do with these flimsy cardboard advertisements. You are inducted. Advertisements that meant nothing to you last week are now your last hope. Look above their scalps. That is salvation up there and maybe a poem.

Only after a while does he notice her and give up his seat to the elderly lady. The pregnant lady, the man with the leg injury. His unfortunate good manners. Scooch over. Scooch away from the smelly wino. It's just a piece of candy wrapper but no one touches it for fear that it contains the world and so one empty seat on the crowded subway car. Spying an empty seat but when you get there soda sloshes. At the next stop someone sits in it and he feels bad for not warning him but that's not his job really. Realization drains into the man's face as the soda leaks through: now there are two seats wet. A vehicular library. Bibles and bestsellers keep away the other citizens' faces. Newspapers in foreign languages cater to communities. Accidentally touch the underside of the seat and become an advocate for stricter gum laws. Halfway to the interview she notices two typos in her résumé. The man on her right snoozes amid the jolts and leans his head on her shoulder as if he sensed her angelhood. Too polite, she resorts to ineffectual nudges. It's kind of funny, actually. The woman across the car smiles at her plight. At the next station he awakes mysteriously and bolts.

Do not hold the doors, do not lean against the doors, the doors are not your friend. If you want friends start a club based on mutual interests, do not come into the subway. He is perfectly attired save for his socks, which mark and doom him when he crosses his legs. The homeless man hopes the next car will be more generous. The musician with the broken trumpet irritates. People examine the scuff marks on their shoes when he walks by with his cup. You reach into your pocket for change but forgot you used it on that phone call and isn't it awkward with that guy sticking his hand out. Folding his coat on his lap to hide the sudden inexplicable erection.

Out of the tunnel and suddenly elevated. Second-floor city. Looking into apartments, browsing lives and what people throw up on their walls. There are never any people in the apartments. Scores of tenement tableaux registering on the eye mostly as moods, mostly sad and blue. He can see through the windows into the next car and wonders if they are happy in there. Cars start off at the same station and then diverge. Two different lines with estranged termini, kin despite complicated parentage. And they're off. His car takes an early lead, a window length and then through struts the competition surges ahead. His car catches up. They meet eyes. Their expressions do not change. This place has practiced them in stuffing down weakness. And then that other car begins its submarine dive here, the tracks go deeper into the earth on their own secret route, west or north, no time for farewells. Let's call it a draw. There's always next time.

A percentage about to get off stands too soon. About to get off but jumped the gun and it's all black out there. Vaguely embarrassed. Their seats are already filled. Should he switch here, he wonders, as the cars pull in to existential station. Run. They all dash out to the local, some come the other way to the express, in rare cases transfers end up taking each other's seats on the other train. It happens less frequently with these modern cars, on these modern tracks, but sometimes the lights go out and what do you do then with all these monsters beside you. I remember when this used to cost a dime. If this car were suddenly transported to a desert island and they were like stuck there she could maybe make out with that guy. Why are you standing so close to me. Is he trying to read the map behind her or interviewing her scalp: you make the call. Here it is, the class trip in their identical day camp T-shirts. Peppy adults herd and hector. Everybody stick together. Pick a buddy. Have you once again picked the car with class trip. Stuck here with these midget mewling things. Too young for sex they punch each other in the arm.

We are stuck in the tunnel on account of a police action at the station ahead of us. We are stuck in the tunnel on account of a sick passenger on the train in front of us. Him again, that rheumy bitch. For someone so sick, he sure gets around a lot. Perhaps he is merely more evolved and now allergic to filth and speed. Take up a collection to subsidize a private limo for the sick passenger. The announcer tried to give information. Every mishap down here radiates outside this car, generating excuses arguments likely stories. What happens down here fertilizes that up-top world. There are slim walkways for mole employees to walk on without being crushed. They have day-glo vests and a deep longing for those who rush by. They get paid to be subterranean. To know what it is to work down there. She finds grit in her fingernails as she speeds past them.

Straphanging actually an antiquated term. It's all metal now, swiveling commas, poles in perpendicular arrangements. But they still hang, still droop, dangle on curled fingers. Feet next to feet. The pole is sickeningly warm God forbid moist from previous fingers. Microbes rejoice. His hand slides slowly down the pole, touching her fingers, so she bids her fingers retreat. He chases, they bump again, she retreats farther. Their hands slide down, all without eye contact. One of many daily contests here. Beware of frottage. Readjust your balance at every lurch. If you don't know what time it is, wait for a peek when he changes his grip. Even if they pulled into his station right now it would be too late.

His heart speeds up before his mind can process the fear: haven't they been between stations for too long. Stationless for quite a while now and it is quite disconcerting. Suddenly realizing you've taken the express. Past familiar stations, farther than you have ever gone before. Neighborhoods you have heard of but never reckoned. Burrowing under a river, good God the horror of a whole different borough. It could be apocalypse above for all you know and who wouldn't think disaster, stuck in the tunnel like that. Isn't this slope just a little too deep. Going down. They have laid rail into the center of the earth and this is where we are going. There are tales of phantom lines, haunted stations. We've all sped past ghost stations where the exits have been bricked up and graffiti warns in looping letters. Abandon all hope. There is no escape if the train stops at ghost stations and we will mill in purgatory. That explains it: he died today without knowing and now this train is taking him to the underworld. Then you suddenly pull in and have to pay again to switch.

They rock in unison, at least they agree on that one small thing. Check their wallets—the demonstrations won't jibe. Review their prayers—the names of their gods won't match. What they cherish and hold dear, their ideals and shopping lists, are as different and numerous as their destinations. But all is not lost. Look around, they're doing a little dance now in the subway car and without rehearsal they all rock together. Shudder and lurch together to the car's orchestrations. Some of them even humming. Everybody's in this together until the next stop, when some of them will get off and some others get on. This is your stop. Get off. Get off now and hurry, before you are trapped in the underworld.

Colson Whitehead was born and raised in New York City. He is the author of The Intuitionist and John Henry Days and is a recipient of a Whiting Award and a MacArthur Fellowship. He lives in Brooklyn.

From *The Colossus of New York: A City in Thirteen Parts.* By Colson Whitehead, copyright © 2003 by Colson Whitehead. Used by permission of Doubleday, a division of Random House, Inc.

STRAPHANGER
DOPPELGÄNGER

Robert Lanham

M iya saw him every morning on the subway platform. They were on the same train schedule. They both rode the L into the city from Brooklyn at 9:15 a.m. "You should ride into Manhattan with me some time," she said to me. "He will freak you the fuck out."

She was right.

Ever since seeing *The Shining*, I've been afraid of identical twins. You know, because they're weird. They have secrets. Being forced to cohabitate with another person inside a dank, 98-degree, one-bedroom uterus does something ungodly to the psyche. Just look at the Olsens.

Given my twin-phobia, one can understand my anxiety when Miya, my close friend and ex-roommate, confessed to numerous sightings of my nonbiological twin. My doppelgänger. He resembled some weird amalgamation of Jon Voight, circa *Midnight Cowboy*, and the guy with the unfortunate bangs from *Logan's Run*. "He looks just like you," she said. "He even has your gut and bad posture." And evidently, this doppelgänging imposter had the nerve to take up residence in my neighborhood. Miya caught the train one subway stop away from my own.

I've seen some pretty weird shit on the subway. A man wearing a jumpsuit made entirely of tin cans on the A train. A woman giving a hand job on the F. A woman wearing an I ♥ Vin Diesel T-shirt on the Q. Tourists who actually give money to that annoying subway performer who bangs on plastic buckets. But the thought of some imposter who looked just like me showing up on the New York public transit system shook me to the core. I decided I'd have to kill him. Or at least do a little detective work to ensure he wasn't making me look bad. After all, if he had the audacity to walk around looking like my twin, he at least better not be doing anything stupid.

According to mythology, a doppelgänger is the living incarnation of a person's dark side. Their shadowy opposite. In translation from the Germanic, the word literally means one's "double goer."

Reflecting on what my dark twin would be like conjured up terrifying images. Did my doppelgänger subscribe to *FHM* instead of the *New Yorker*? Did he wear shell necklaces and listen to rap metal? Did he enjoy movies made by Jerry Bruckheimer? Was his idea of a good time an all-inclusive vacation package at a Sandals Caribbean resort? Did he think dreadlocks looked good on white people? Was he praying for a Jeb Bush ticket in the 2008 presidential election?

I began having doppelgänger anxiety. After all, if my doppelgänger was making unfortunate life decisions, it could it reflect poorly on me. What if a colleague, thinking it was me, spotted him cruising through the Village on a skateboard? What if he routinely visited peep shows outside the Port Authority? Or worse, what if he's one of those people who carries a ferret with him everywhere in a backpack?

Coming to terms with the existence of your nonbiological twin is part of living in New York. In a city this size, everyone is bound to have one. My friend Sara, for instance, was accosted by a group of giggling strangers who insisted upon taking her picture. They worked with Sara's doppelgänger on Wall Street. My friend Larry, who works at a gallery in Chelsea, has a doppelgänger as well. My wife and I call him Brownbag Larry whenever we see him, because he's prone to clutching a lunch bag.

Nevertheless, I've yet to meet anyone who actually knows his or her own shadowy double. Perhaps fate does its best to prohibit such encounters. According to traditional folklore, if two doppelgängers are to meet, they both will die.

Regardless, our meeting seemed inevitable. He was on the same subway line as me and evidently lived just blocks away. Maybe it wouldn't be so bad having a twin, I tried to convince myself. We could buy matching sweatsuits and play racquetball together. We could make some extra cash in a Doublemint commercial. We could play practical jokes on friends and senile relatives.

But try as I might, I couldn't get used to the idea of having a twin. It just made me feel cheap. And perhaps I've watched too many horror films, but I kept envisioning him standing over my bed in the dead of night with a hatchet.

One night, my wife received a call from a friend with whom she'd recently lost touch. Turns out, "I" had just been spotted gallivanting around Manhattan with a curvaceous young blonde. Thankfully, I had a good alibi, since I was having dinner with my wife when the call was placed. Weeks prior, a friend had reprimanded me for not speaking to him on a subway platform that I had never set foot on. "I guess you were distracted by that cute brunette you were with," he said.

I decided the time had come to have a conversation with this alter egotist who was whoring himself all over town with my good looks. Nevertheless, the idea of meeting him made me nervous. I'd seen *Vertigo* and *Dead Ringers*. More important, I didn't want to spend much time with someone whose very presence could bring about my untimely demise. If the opportunity presented itself, I decided, I would follow him. Albeit from afar.

Several weeks ago I awoke before dawn, sweating and with a fever. At the time, I was juggling numerous writing deadlines and avoiding several editors' phone calls. I was secretly delighted to be under the weather. Illness was the perfect excuse to take a break.

Lying awake in bed, I watched all the early morning shows and soon found myself anxious and fidgety. The chemistry between Katie Couric and Matt Lauer has that effect on me. I decided I'd turn off the TV and stroll over to Miya's house. She was out of town and I'd agreed to watch her cats. She'd adopted them from a relative who'd recently died. I'd yet to meet them.

Miya hadn't mentioned it, but her cats, Gina and Beatrice, were both tabbies. They were virtually indistinguishable. In a note tacked to her door she instructed that Gina, "the fatter one," needed to be given a pill. They both looked fat to me. The only discernible difference I noticed between Gina and Beatrice was that one was able to draw blood when it swatted. I tried calling Miya's cell phone to find out which cat needed the pill, but the call went straight to her mailbox.

Frustrated that I'd have to come back later after hearing from Miya, I decided to skip the pill and just serve the pointy-eared devils their dollops of Fancy Feast. I didn't want to take the chance on giving a pill to the "less fat one." More important, I didn't want to get scratched again. (I selected the Whitefish & Egg Blend for the cat with the bloody claws, while the nicer one got the Gourmet Salmon Blend.)

In hindsight, I realize I should have seen my unpleasant interaction with the matching felines as an omen. But I was too busy applying direct pressure to my flesh wounds to give it much thought.

I'd begun to feel feverish again, so I decided to take the train home one stop instead of walking. I sat down on the subway bench in the middle of the Bedford Avenue platform and waited for the train to arrive. That's when it happened. I spotted him. My doppel-gänger was leaning nonchalantly against a post at the far end of the platform, distracted by a book he was reading. I felt my adrenaline flowing. It was eerie. The resemblance was striking, but there were subtle differences nonetheless. His face was rounder. His eyes more sunken. He was a smart casual to my harebrained unkempt. And to my dismay, he preferred pleats. All doubts that he was my double were erased when I noticed he was reading a Lance Armstrong biography. I hate sports. It was precisely the title my polar opposite would select.

Since I didn't feel well enough to get any work done anyway, I decided to follow him.

He took the L train three stops to Union Square, where he transferred to the northbound Q train. My daily commute, I realized, was the opposite of his. I had an office in Tribeca and generally transferred to the southbound Q train.

I followed him at a safe distance, careful not to be spotted. Still too engrossed by his book to notice I was stalking him, he rode the train two more stops before exiting at 42nd Street. Poor soul, I thought. He worked in midtown. But since he was supposed to be my inverse, perhaps he preferred being surrounded by tourists and having overpriced poppers for lunch at one of the countless midtown chains. Or maybe he enjoyed being close to the nearby Disney store where he could buy identical Lion King panties for the curvaceous blonde and the cute brunette.

I followed him as he crossed Broadway and made his way into a Starbucks. I waited outside at a newsstand. I was curious what he would order, deducing that my opposite would probably prefer a decaf with Splenda®. And as I waited, I wondered where he would work. Was he an accountant at Morgan Stanley? Did he fetch donuts for Graydon Carter when the *Vanity Fair* editor needed his afternoon sugar fix?

As I was pondering these questions, he exited, and I resumed my stalk.

Several blocks north of the Starbucks, I found myself standing a few feet behind him as he waited for a streetlight to change. I wanted to get close enough to see which boxes were checked on his

Starbucks cup, and for some reason, I wanted to smell him. That's when something terrifying happened. Perhaps sensing my presence, he looked over his shoulder right at me. I'd been discovered.

The encounter only lasted a moment, but it seemed much longer at the time. When our eyes met, he seemed startled. I suddenly realized that he'd assuredly heard about me as well. As he looked me up and down, I felt self-conscious. Competitive. I sucked my gut in and wondered if my hair looked OK. I felt like a weird approximation of myself. A Lunchbag Larry. Inexplicably, I wanted to arm wrestle.

As his eyes returned once again to my own, he let out a barely audible "hmmm." Then he turned and crossed the street shaking his head. I felt diminished. A ghost of myself. I stood there loutishly for a moment, wondering what to make of his ambiguous reaction, before I noticed he'd disappeared.

Feeling drained, I decided I'd stop by the coffee shop to order a double espresso before taking the subway back home. Caffeine was probably the last thing I needed since I was sick, but my encounter had deflated me. I'd noticed my doppelgänger was in better shape than me, so I decided against sugar in favor of Splenda®. Foods that require trademarks must be better than the boring, run-of-the-mill, old-fashioned type, I deduced.

I descended back down into the subway with my cup in hand and passed a subway performer who danced to salsa music with a life-size, strangely Aryan doll. I'd seen him before and his act had always struck me as fetishistic. Oddly disturbing. Years ago, I'd seen the performer having a drink in the now-defunct Siberia bar—a dark and gritty dive inside the 1/9 station at 50th Street. His doll was perched in the adjacent bar seat. I wondered if someone as bizarre as this man had a doppelgänger too. Perhaps a subway artist who performed a Riverdance routine in the London Undergound with a curvaceous doll dressed in lederhosen.

I made my way to the southbound Q platform, where there was a small crowd, mainly tourists, waiting for the train. I was relieved that rush hour had ended. The train rolled into the station with a screech and I boarded. As I entered the car, I noticed it was empty, save a spilled Starbucks cup on the far end. No one else was in the car. I sat down, perplexed. An empty subway car in Manhattan is an anomaly. It was quiet inside, devoid of its usual hum. Then I figured it out. The air-conditioning wasn't working. The riders had moved to contingent cars to escape the heat. My fever had increased, so the warmth felt good to me. I decided to stay where I was. Millions of people ride the subway every day, I realized, yet I'd managed to find the one empty car in Manhattan. I was happy to be alone with myself.

Robert Lanham *is the author of the beach-towel classic* The Emerald Beach Trilogy *which includes the titles* Pre-Coitus, Coitus, *and* Aftermath. *More recent works include* Food Court Druids, Cherohonkees, and Other Creatures Unique to the Republic, *and* The Hipster Handbook. *Lanham's writing has appeared in* The New York Times, Nylon, The Washington Post, Playboy, *and* Time Out. *He is currently working on a new book about Evangelical Christianity in America. He is the editor and founder of www.freewilliamsburg.com and lives in Brooklyn, New York.*

TRANSFER

Leigh Stolle

It could have been his hands, tough old baseball mitts. Or her glasses, big bifocalled panes extending from mid-cheek to above her penciled brows. Or perhaps it was how they stood, their arms vined around the steel poles, their legs stiff against the rhythm of the train. The two together, but not touching.

Despite what they'd been told, they mooned at faces that wouldn't return their gaze. In fact they broke many rules: They carefully read the advertisements posted overhead. They bent to watch the 4 and 5 trains zip past on the other side. They quietly clutched their belongings when people entered their space.

Then there was their age, a factor they could neither hide nor would want to, but which set them apart all the same. They were children of the Depression, a breed increasingly seldom seen, and especially not around Astor Place, entering a New York subway train at rush hour.

These were the clues that would have signaled

"tourists" to the others on the 6 train, lower-Manhattan–bound, that cool October morning—if the others had cared to notice. If they hadn't already slid into that meditative place subway riders go when en route and alone. Despite the couple's desire to blend—they'd been coached on all the dos and don'ts—they were indubitably, conspicuously, not from here. And not only were they tourists, but what particular brand was also clear: Midwesterners. This brand was discernible even to native New Yorkers who'd never ventured across the Mississippi. One could practically see the snap peas and golden wheat and beef steaks woven into their very flesh—solid limbs and postures, ruddy cheeks, though hers genteelly powdered. Nearly as conspicuous as their unflagging health was a conviction that, while NYC was a fascinating place to visit, there could be no place like home.

"Stand clear of the closing doors, please," the officious announcer instructed, and the couple, who seemed comforted by the voice in this city of strangers, drew closer to their pole.

At their fiftieth anniversary dinner the previous fall, the couple's children—my three older sisters and I—had presented them with a choice of trips: a tour of Germany, a cabin in the Rockies, an Alaskan cruise, or a Hawaiian escape.

For months they demurred. They were not good at accepting gifts, especially from their children.

"You kids can't afford it," our father said.

"Pick," we replied, too busy with our own adult lives to beg.

"But everything we love is right here," our mother reasoned.

"Pick," we warned.

"But the money . . ."

"Pick!" we commanded, taking pleasure in the role-reversal and license to use the imperative in the name of good intentions.

"But the cats . . ."

"Pick or I will!" shrieked the oldest, who'd never forgiven them for having her first.

Cowed, they chose. Individually, and to different daughters, in off-the-record kinds of conversations, they confided their holiday dreams.

"Germany," our father said, a twinkle in his eye. Then, with throat cleared, "Or wherever your mother wants to go."

"Hawaii," our mother whispered, smiling. Then soberly, "Or wherever your father wants to go."

Then in a chain reaction predictable but not foreseen, upon learning the other's choice, each seized up, and refused to go to either place. And from opposite directions they galloped like old ponies back to the safety of their stable of excuses, adding: Our suitcases are too ratty! Who'll baby-sit? and such.

Winter passed, spring breezed by, and summer was in repose when in a moment of not altogether disingenuous goodwill toward my siblings, all of whom lived within drop-in range of parents, I entered a plucky dark horse: Why not send them my way, to New York City? And to ease their minds, I puffed with a whiff of self-righteousness, I'd be their guide.

Touched and anxious at once, our parents said "Yes. Why yes!" But then they remembered what a mean, rebellious teen I had been. And because they weren't sure, they asked, "Are you sure?"

And I said, "Sure!" though I still resented them for that bag of weed they'd thrown into the wood-burning stove.

Then silently we each vowed to behave, and waited like leaves for the autumn day to come.

Somewhere between Bleecker and Spring, my father, his farmer's tan a permanent stain of brown from his collar up and shirtsleeves down, shared a smile with a stranger who'd stepped on with a child. The toddler hugged his father's leg as the stranger allowed a courtesy smile, which my father read as opportunity and, without a beat, tossed out some patter about the child, which the urbanite seemed not unhappy to entertain.

Since my parents' arrival three days earlier, my father had, with no small effort, adhered to his daughters' admonishment to avoid needless conversing with strangers. But today, day three of four, he was ready to spread his wings, and soon guided the conversation to the very thing they were racing toward: a visit to Ellis Island. As he told the stranger of his own father's arrival to New York from a north German town nearly a century before, he intuitively poked a callused finger through the train's darkened windows toward the island's locale off Manhattan's southwest tip. This despite his own location dozens of feet underground and nearly 1,300 miles from the rural town where he and the woman had roosted since 1960 in a modest ranch-style house atop a two-acre hill. True, he'd been to New York before, just prior to his service overseas. He remembered touring the Empire State Building with some army buddies, he said, gesturing back north toward the landmark's famous tower. But little else, he said with a wave. He imagined a lot had changed since then.

The stranger nodded and let a brief silence hang as the 6 surged down the track. Then, with the next stop his own, he asked the pair where they were visiting from.

"Oh, Kansas," my father said, this time pointing west.

Now the others took notice. People who would fail to hear a live mariachi band working the car were suddenly curious about this duo. And while my father did tend to speak loudly—he'd lost some hearing over the years, tended to shout on the phone. And his gestures on the subway had been rather broad, reckless in a place of space economy. There could be no doubt that what had turned the straphangers into rubberneckers was the K-word: *Kansas*.

I watched the exchange from my seat some feet away, too tired from three days of tour-guiding to stand. The riders' reaction was a physiological phenomenon familiar to me and every other native of the state. To say "Kansas" was to wish a titter from a stranger, be she heel or sophisticate. "Really?" the person would stall, then search for a seemingly sensitive follow-up. "So, your family still lives there?" *You're related to people who live there . . . by choice?* they'd mean. To which I had a rotation of responses, including, "Kansas is where I grew up, yes. But whether it's where I was *created* or *evolved* remains to be seen." I wondered what words my German grandfather, in his Old World clothes and thick accent, had used to defend his home.

To the others in the car, my father's friendliness seemed a forgivable enough subway-culture transgression if only for the genuine exuberance with which he shared his and his wife's plans. Today, he explained, they hoped to confirm that his father had arrived by steamship in 1913 at the age of fourteen, as the family's genealogical notes had it. The teenager had traveled from New York to Nebraska, where an uncle and German community awaited him. Later, spurred by the desire to master English, he left the community and headed south for the rolling hills of eastern Kansas. There he bought a square of farmland and a boxcar to live in, started a family, and called it home.

Ellis Island, however, was just one of many stops on the couple's trip, my father continued. A trip planned by their daughters, my mother would have added had the conversation been less public. One a teacher, one a nurse, one in sales, and one our personal guide, she'd have said, smiling over the rims of her glasses at me. Four daughters. Four girls in all.

In fact, from the early '60s to the late '70s, in a rural corner of Silver Lake, Kansas, it had been all girls, all up and down a graveled stretch of 35th Street. There was the first generation: The Brumbaugh girls (Julie, Judy, and Connie). The Martin girls (Peggy, Karen, Diane, and Nancy). And of course the couple's own brood (Barbara, Brenda, Kimberly, and Kathleen). Then the baby boomer round followed: The McIntire girls (Robin and Chelsea). The Krueger girls (Tammy, Christy, and Jenny). And the Robinson girls (Raquel, Kimbre, and Lacey). Must be something in the well water, locals joked so often as to maybe have even secretly believed it, what with Roswell, Bay of Pigs, and Watergate looming in the conservative community's collective mind. Eventually, however, county water lines were laid, little boys were had, and the oddity was spoiled.

As I watched my parents converse with the stranger, I felt a tug of pride. Proud of the joie de vivre with which they'd tackled the city. In fact, their tourist zeal—including the nervous thrill they got from taking the subway—had become almost infectious, threatening to transfer to me. Though I myself usually walked, drawing energy from the blue swaths of sky and climbing ivy and even fresh-cut flower stands, I appreciated the convenience of traversing the city underground. And over months of hosting family, friends, and the intermittent boyfriend, I'd developed a love of the efficacy with which it facilitated swift—and thereby relatively painless—good-byes. *Good to see them come,* I recalled from a favorite John Gorka song. *A little better to see them go.*

That wasn't to say I didn't enjoy a lengthy ride. One of my favorite chakra-cleansing New York routes was the meditative E-from-Jamaica-Center-to-the-6-at-51st-from-JFK-fresh-off-the-redeye-from-Denver, a journey I would use to analyze the wisdom of maintaining a certain rocky, long-distance romance.

I'd ridden a similarly long route on a daily basis while living in Paris, where I'd gone one fall to learn French and heal from a recent breakup. The language school was near Place Saint-Michel on the lip of the Seine's left bank, while my host family resided in the 20th arrondissement on the right bank, nearly forty minutes away by metro. It was a daydream-filled commute, my mind left to roam at the start and finish of each day. Coursework comprised the typical morning feature, while clips from the breakup were the popular late matinee. To be in Paris in autumn with a broken heart was, I concluded, a sickeningly beautiful thing. Like spilled blood, ghastly and exquisite at once.

Of me and my sisters, three of us were single—an admittedly anomalous state given the traditional milieu in which we'd been raised. I was grateful my parents didn't identify my sisters and me by "family status," like so many of their generation did. *That's Ron, who's married with two darling . . .* Our parents had never pressured us to marry. If you're happy, we're happy, they said, though our mother would on occasion, in a form of reflective therapy, ask us privately if their marriage—as void of affection as it was of conflict—was the reason we'd chosen to stay single.

"Yes," we'd deadpan. "You taught us well."

At Brooklyn Bridge–City Hall, the 6 line terminated, my parents and I stepped off, and confusion stepped in. A transfer during rush hour. They hadn't expected this. It wasn't so complicated. A simple change of trains across the platform, from the 6 to the 4 train. It was just that they hadn't planned for it. Had been caught off guard. *Never let your guard down*, their daughters had coached. They were planners, especially my mother, who kept a calendar by the wall phone in the kitchen and scheduled events on the spot, the phone cradled against her collarbone, her hands writing in neat script *Washburn girls b-ball, 5:30 p.m.; Church meeting, 7 p.m.* In fact, as she did on every vacation, she'd brought a tiny notepad on the trip, marking down names of famous buildings and dates of historic events and related private thoughts, all of which she'd review once home and see what a wonderful time she had.

But this moment she'd have to note later. The transfer was disorienting. People in their strangeness brushing and shoving, making physical contact. My parents seldom touched friends or neighbors or even each other for that matter, let alone perfect strangers. Yet here they were, bumping quarters like sheep, bottlenecking at the 4 train's closing doors.

Already aboard I beckoned them to follow. And so my mother—who could be surprisingly aggressive—charged ahead, squeezing onto the 4 with the masses, expecting her husband to follow. But my father, who subscribed to a kind of global chivalry (extended to both sexes, to anyone younger or older, to weaker or smaller, to, in short, anyone perceived less manly than he) deferred for the several seconds it took the car to compact. That no part of his 200-pound frame could reasonably fit was a realization he and my mother, who now stood several people deep into the car, her eyes just clearing someone's shoulder, arrived at in unison. It was a shared, controlled panic in which words on the verge of being uttered were clipped by the subway bell. *Ding*. Then the doors glided shut, separating the tourists with polite efficiency.

Still on the platform stood my father, wearing an impish grin of resignation. A trip to Germany it wasn't, but an adventure nonetheless.

Through the glass I mouthed, "Fulton Street! Fulton Street!" pointing in the direction the train had begun to move. But my father, squinting through his smudged glasses, simply shrugged and grinned and waved good-bye. Behind me, my mother stood with her hands—the backs a bony relief map of blue veins and brown dots—pressed to her cheeks, her green eyes excited with worry.

For a moment, I shared my mother's anxiety, the unexpected separation triggering in each of us, first a primitive urge to rejoin the pack, then a cranial surge to *think! think! think!*

I imagined my father at the ticket window, stammering as he did when excited, hunched down explaining his predicament through the exchange slot. He'd then scowl through the glass, through the commotion, through the MTA worker's Gambian or Dominican or Brooklyn accent, not catching a word of the reply. But he was resourceful. The original MacGyver (a workshop full of vises and antlers and bass lures and epoxy and old socks to prove it), and at seventy-three, he was beyond spry; he was robust. And could easily have walked—high-kicked!—the rest of the way to Battery Park had he chosen to. He would have preferred it, in fact—a chance to explore more of the city, chat up a vendor or two, add to his socio-cultural observations, which he collected and spun into colorful tales by which their vacations had become known. But instead, of course, he would try to catch up, my mother and I reasoned, logic now back in command. We agreed to step off at the next platform and see what the next train would bring.

At Fulton Street station, the plan was executed with aplomb. The

4 pulled in. My father was aboard. The doors slid open. And mother and daughter jumped in.

But then something unscripted happened. My parents, in an exuberant reunion, embraced in a way I'd never witnessed. It was a loving, almost passionate, squeeze, with my mother happily burying her face in my father's chest, an arm soothing her husband's broad back, he with both arms in an assuring bear hug around her. They beamed at each other and around the car, my mother's hands and feet doing a giddy little dance all about her man, her voice twitting sweetly at him like a swallow.

Now, no question, New Yorkers were staring. Including me, one hand covering my mouth. I could almost channel my mother's giddiness, so palpable it was making me dizzy. And the tenderness of my father allowing himself to enjoy the moment—I gripped a pole with my free hand, eyes still fixed on the spectacle. The train had become an amusement park ride. These weren't the people who raised me. Had we all stepped onto a Frank Capra set? Was Norman Rockwell aboard with an easel and paint?

To outsiders, they no doubt appeared to be a silly tourist couple having a holiday squeeze. But I had reason to stare. In thirty-eight years I'd never witnessed such genuine affection between my parents. Were they simply in the throes of a vacation-induced romantic flourish? Or, after fifty years of stalwart partnership, had a little joy—somewhere along the way, sometime after the nest had emptied—blossomed?

I stared on with a woozy mix of glee and envy. How could I be seeing something that I grew up believing didn't exist? I felt my magnetic north altering.

Out into the crisp morning air, I ushered my parents through Battery Park, past peddlers of handbags and watches and gold. Ahead their ferry bobbed, loading a steady parade of tourists. My parents chirped at the sight of the bay and the Statue of Liberty in the distant haze, and once in line cheerfully waved me good-bye.

My office, at Houston and Varick, was a brisk fifteen-minute walk away, direction northwest. But instead I ambled eastward, the sun at my face, descending at South Ferry station. From there I'd ride a slow 1/9 and let myself be transported.

Leigh Stolle worked as a journalist before earning an MFA in creative writing from Emerson College. She currently lives on the Upper East Side of Manhattan and is working on a collection of short stories.

UNDER THE SKIN

Yona Zeldis McDonough

Wanda and I come clattering down the stairs of the subway station at 7th Avenue and Flatbush in Brooklyn. It's a little after three o'clock on a winter afternoon and we've just gotten out of school. We reach the turnstiles and put in our tokens before descending a second set of stairs, this time to the platform itself. A train has just left the station; the people who have gotten off pass us on the stairs. There will be a wait, maybe a long one, for the next train. But we have time and are not worried.

Wanda and I are on our way to Manhattan for our respective ballet lessons; she attends the Joffrey School on Sixth Avenue and Tenth Street, while I take class in a small studio on West Fifty-sixth Street. The day is surprisingly mild, and I am hot in my coat—a new, brown shearling with a soft black collar, a gift from my doting grandparents—but I don't take it off, because I don't want to carry it. I am already lugging a multipocketed canvas dance bag that holds not only my schoolbooks, but two pairs of ballet slippers, practice clothes, and all the paraphernalia needed to turn my long mass of dark hair into a sleek, tightly coiled bun. There is no train in sight yet, so Wanda and I sit down on the platform's bench and set our bulging bags—hers is as overstuffed as mine—by our feet. A few other people trickle down the stairs to join us, but the platform is long and poorly lit; our fellow travelers seem to disperse into the shadows and we remain alone on the bench, deeply engrossed in the things fourteen-year-old budding ballerinas talk about.

This is the second year I have been allowed to take the subway into "the city" (as we Brooklyn girls are wont to call it) by myself and now that I attend class five afternoons a week as well as Saturday morning, I am on the subway a lot. This is a time, the early 1970s, when the city's fortunes seem imperiled and the subway system reflects the general shabbiness and decline that is everywhere. Stations are dirty and poorly maintained; trains arrive spottily and are subject to frequent breakdowns. There is graffiti on many of the cars, which are old, and in the summer, they are stifling because they are seldom air-conditioned. None of this matters a jot to me. I love the subways, the freedom they offer, their range and scope and speed. The subways make me feel connected—like an animate and pulsating dot on the subway map I am fond of studying—to the vast and wonderful city that has only begun to open itself up for me. I can begin my journey underground in Brooklyn, and emerge into the radiant light of so many new, compelling places: Greenwich Village, where I shop at the Capezio store on MacDougal Street and slurp down an Orange Julius on Eighth; Lincoln Center, where for two dollars I can buy student rush tickets to see Balanchine's three-act wonder, *Jewels*; the Cloisters, where I walk through a vernal, leafy, park in search of unicorns, which I find, albeit in two-dimensional woven form, hanging on the walls of the fortresslike museum that houses them.

It's not that I'm unaware of the subway's problems or its potential dangers—I have already experienced the shock of feeling a strange man's erect penis pressing against my hip in a crowded car, the appalled sorrow of seeing the leathery, bare feet and oozing skin rash of a homeless woman as she shuffles along the platform of the 34th Street station—but somehow these things don't touch me, not really. I am young, I ardently believe in my own talent and promise, and I hold up my trusting, well-intentioned heart as a shield or talisman against all possible harm. I don't wish to hurt anyone else, I dumbly reason. Why would anyone want to hurt me?

Wanda reaches for her dance bag to pull out a snack—a cup of Dannon strawberry yogurt—and pries off the top. She eats it quickly and gets up to deposit the empty container in the overflowing trash basket. Her bag remains on the platform, pushed slightly under the bench. I decide to check my own bag for something to eat—I usually carry a box of raisins or a piece of fruit—and to gain better access to its contents, I pull it to my lap. I have just located an orange buried in its depths when three black girls appear. One is heavyset and wears a bright pink jacket with a big dark stain—Ink? Magic marker?—on the arm; another is tiny and elfin, her hair arranged in a series of complicated braids that stand out from her head like exclamation points; the third is light-skinned and slender in an oversized camel coat, and when I first lay eyes on her, I think that she looks like a ballet dancer. They are laughing and pushing one another when they first step into view, but now that they see us—a pair of white girls seemingly alone on the platform—they stop and fall silent. I can sense that something is about to happen, though I cannot tell yet what it is. But I understand that our presence—white, entitled, on our own—is somehow perceived as a kind of challenge.

It is Wanda who makes the first move back to the bench to reach for her bag. The heavy girl in pink gets there first. She seizes the bag and raises it up into the air above her head.

"Give that back," says Wanda. She sounds tentative, frightened. I don't blame her. I am frightened too. What do these girls want from us? Our bags? Our money? Or is it something less tangible and more complicated than that?

"Why should I?" the girl asks. She is shaking the bag this way and that. A small wad of tissues falls to the platform, and the tiny girl kicks at it until it has gone over the edge, onto the tracks.

"Because it's mine."

"Not anymore. Finders keepers, losers weepers," the girl says. She continues to swing the bag around, and more things tumble out—a comb, a brush, and a packet of bobby pins that scatter like confetti as they land. The girls snicker as Wanda kneels down and tries, unsuccessfully, to gather up her belongings. Something about her frantic, scrabbling gesture galvanizes me out of my fear and paralysis. I stand, clutching my own bag firmly under my arm.

"Stop it or I'm going to tell." My voice sounds squeaky and ineffectual; still I have to try.

"Tell?" The big girl swivels around to look at me. "Who you gonna tell?"

"The token clerk," I say and head for the stairs. I am frightened but angered, too, and I feel my face heat in righteous indignation. My body, though, is trembling, and I am grateful to wrap my hand around the worn wood of the railing.

"You do that, I'll throw the bag on the tracks."

"No, we'll throw her on the tracks." This comment is offered by the tiny girl. Her teeth are very even and white; she has a small dimple in one cheek.

"Both of you. Both of you—on the tracks," says the one who looks like a ballerina. Her voice is low, but menacing.

I stop, unsure of what to do next. I want to race upstairs, find an adult who will help us, rescue us. But I am afraid of leaving Wanda alone with these girls. I have no frame of reference with which to understand their malice. Why do they want to taunt us, even hurt us? What could inspire such feelings, such acts? Although race divides us, isn't the fact that we are all girls—soon to be women—something that should unite us? Now something else infects my fear: betrayal. Although I have never seen these girls before in my life, I still feel as if they have betrayed me, betrayed our entire gender. It all feels like too much and without warning, the potent, confusing brew of my emotion erupts in a flood of spontaneous tears. I sit down on the filthy subway platform and sob, sob as if my heart is breaking, which, in a way, it is.

Suddenly, the platform is swarming with people.

"What's going on here?" says a man with a briefcase and tweed jacket.

"Are you all right?" asks a woman in a dark red suit.

Wanda offers a jumbled, somewhat incoherent version of our plight; I am crying too hard to say anything.

The man with the briefcase admonishes the girls. The heavy one and the graceful one look down at their shoes, but the tiny one says, "We were just teasing. We wasn't gonna hurt them." I continue to cry.

"Do you want me to call your parents?" says the woman in red, kindly.

"What about something to drink?" says another woman, this one with gray hair, a large flowered handbag, and thick-soled, orthopedic shoes. "A soda? A cup of tea?" She rummages around in her back and produces a roll of LifeSavers. I take one but instead of putting it in my mouth, I clutch it in my hand, where it quickly grows sticky. I bury it in the pocket of my new coat, where I know it will fester like a small rank sore, but I don't care.

The subway train comes pounding into the station and we are all momentarily quiet. It slows to a stop and the doors open. All of us—the three girls, Wanda, the two women, the man, and I—get on. The black girls move off to one end of the car while Wanda and I remain near the adults who have been our saviors.

"Don't worry. I'll ride uptown with you," says the man. "How far are you going?" Wanda tells him our destinations—she plans to get off at the West 4th Street station, while I continue on to the stop at

7th Avenue and 53rd Street. We find seats and he pulls a newspaper out of his briefcase. Wanda and I do not talk, mostly because I am, to my own dismay, still crying, though not as hard now. The train pulls out of the tunnel and out onto the Manhattan Bridge. I love this view—Brooklyn behind us, Manhattan up ahead, the great, gray expanse of water separating the two, and the massive configuration of beams, cables, and arches uniting them again. My crying tapers off and I find myself able to look toward the other end of the car, where the three girls are still sitting. I can see them looking back, wary, puzzled glances that dart our way and then retreat.

"Don't start anything," Wanda says, aware of my gaze.

But it is too late. One of the girls—the tiny one—gets up from her seat and walks toward me. Weak winter sun comes in from the windows, and she steps into a pool of light. When she is standing right in front of me, I reluctantly look up. So does the man seated next to me, but he does not say anything.

"It's like I told you," she begins. "We weren't going to hurt you."

I want to say I know, it's okay, but I don't trust my voice so I just nod.

"So you can stop crying now," she adds.

That does it. I am off again, awash in a river of tears. All the things I want to say to her—*If you didn't mean to hurt us, then why did you act like you did? Why did you want to frighten us? What do you have against us? We have nothing against you; we're all girls, together, don't you see? Sisters under the skin?*—are deluged by my tears, washed away. I could see the man beside me frowning, and the girl retreats to where her friends sit waiting. When she reaches them, she begins talking, quickly it seems, and with lots of hand gestures. She looks back at me once more—a look whose intention I cannot grasp—and then not again.

The train descends, leaving behind the glimpses of water, of city, of sky. Wanda gets off at West 4th Street, with a hug and a murmured promise to call me later. My protector is getting off at 42nd Street. He stands clutching the newspaper under his arm and the briefcase in his hand. He looks over to where the girls still sit, clustered in their tight, impervious knot.

"They won't bother you anymore," he says. "You'll be all right now."

"Thank you," I tell him. "For everything." The doors glide open and he is gone.

The car is filled with people now; I cannot see the girls, who are still sitting at its far end. I have only one more stop before I reach my own destination. The man is right. They will not harm me now; I have no reason to be afraid. And I am not. But I am sad, sad in a way I have never been before but will be, of course, many, many times again.

The train pulls into the station at 7th Avenue and 53rd Street, and I hoist my bag onto my shoulder. I strain for one last glimpse of them—the heavy one in her impossibly pink coat, the tiny one, the ballerina—and for a second I am able to see them, before the doors of the subway open, then close, cutting us off from each other forever.

Yona Zeldis McDonough is the author of the novels The Four Temperaments *and* In Dahlia's Wake *and the editor of the essay collections* The Barbie Chronicles: A Living Doll Turns Forty *and* All the Available Light: A Marilyn Monroe Reader.

Bombs! Anthrax! Gas! Ho, Hum.

Ken Wheaton

It was a balmy Thursday morning in Manhattan. Above ground, clouds rolled in and thunder rumbled. It was going to be one of those miserable August commuting days in which my body, perhaps harboring some sort of instinctual echo, expected the caverns of the subway system to provide refuge from the heat. My mind, of course, knew better. The subway system is not a natural phenomenon. On a muggy summer day, the caves of New York are about as refreshing as a used diaper—just as smelly, twice as damp. And you have to share.

But on this particular morning I was resigned to my fate and was in no way surprised that ten a.m. found me on an uptown 3 train sitting motionless at 34th Street. I was already late but in no rush. The rest of the passengers seemed evenly divided: those who were, like me, late and didn't care and those who were late and tapping their feet, checking their watches. The latter, in turn, were divided into yet another two camps: those who were cursing to themselves and those who were looking for someone to curse. I kept my head down, practiced the ancient subway art of making no eye contact.

A voice came down from on high, clear and strong. It was a miracle! The subway's speakers were working. The conductor spoke clear English: "Ladies and gentlemen, there is a train ahead of us, and we hope to be moving shortly."

But of course.

Just one day, I want the speaker to crackle to life and inform us that, for our undying patience, we've all won some sort of fabulous prize. But no, it's always mysterious delays or sick passengers or signal problems.

He spoke again: "Ladies and gentlemen, this train is no longer in service, and there is no uptown 3 service at this time."

The curses were no longer muttered. Like spoiled and angry children we all stood up and stomped out of the train, most to find an alternate means of transportation, some to stop and pester the conductor.

"Well, what am I supposed to do?!" shouted one passenger. "How am I supposed to get to work?"

It was exactly one week after the London subway bombings on July 7, and it was business as usual on New York subways.

Then again, it wasn't like things were different on the morning of July 7, either. That morning I took the crowded train into work, reading one of the free daily newspapers, iPod earbuds jammed in my ears. Nothing seemed amiss. No one seemed to act like bombs had gone off in London trains hours before. I certainly didn't. But that's because I didn't know about it. I first heard about it when the screen in the elevator in my office building told me that two people had died. Between leaving the elevator and getting to my desk, that number had gone up to thirty.

As far as I could tell, no one riding in the subways that morning had so much as blinked. Maybe they were just too busy thanking the gods that New York had lost the Olympics bid and we'd no longer have to suffer through Mayor Bloomberg telling us how swell it would be to have a million more people funneling into the city during the middle of the summer. New Yorkers heard about subway bombings in London and their response was to walk out the door and commute to work on their own subways. No surprise there.

In the weeks after September 11, there was a great deal of talk about a new spirit of fraternity among city dwellers, people being more polite and considerate. Most of this talk was coming from celebrities. Celebrities debarking from their limousines to take a quick tour of the devastation at Ground Zero practically marveled at people waving at them—*waving,* for the love of God! And offering water to the firemen! And volunteering!

The next year, there was a scene in *Spider-Man* that echoed this. The Goblin, terrorizing New Yorkers on the 59th Street Bridge, was attacked with insults and garbage. "If you mess with one of us, you mess with all of us," yells one portly gentleman.

I shouldn't have to remind anyone that *Spider-Man* was based on a comic book and that the movie was written by Hollywood types, known for doing all sorts of crazy things like taking hallucinogenic drugs, spending twenty dollars on martinis, and signing up for Scientology. But taking the subway? Forget about it.

Sure, I was proud that fellow New Yorkers were pitching in and helping out above ground, but I was also proud that it took all of a week for subterranean New York to get back to normal. And by normal I mean shoving a little old lady in the back to force her into the 5 train so that you could squeeze yourself in there. By normal I mean pretending to sleep so that you don't see the pregnant woman on crutches staring at the top of your head as you sit in the clearly marked "priority seating" while she says just loud enough for you to hear, something about "trifling muthafuckas" and you mutter under your breath, "Let someone else give up his seat."

Not that I'd know anything about that sort of exchange.

Many would attribute this business-as-usual mentality to the tenacity of New Yorkers. We're rude and we've got places to be, so get the hell out of the way. "Yes, even you there, the one with a bomb-jacket strapped around your chest. You make me late for work, and I swear to God I will beat your silly ass."

This same sort of thinking was applied by the Brits immediately after July 7. The stiff upper lip and all that. "We can't very well let something as simple as a few bombs on the Tube muck up the day. It wouldn't be proper. Carry on. It's what we do."

The truth of the matter is that Londoners went back to work the next day and New Yorkers went back to normal, well, because we didn't exactly have a choice. We had no spare car in the garage. Most of us had no garage. And that rent isn't going to pay itself, now is it?

There's something more going on here. Something more than being a New Yorker or a Londoner. It's not about culture at all. It's about conditioning. It's about an endless stream of days spent in a Zen-like state of ignoring the little voices in your head.

We never think about the subway system. Like air and George Steinbrenner, it's just there. But for the purposes of this argument, try to think about it.

Ignore the potential crime, the smell of the bums, the heat (or the cold), the crazy passengers, the crowded conditions. Stick to the essence of the subway. It's one of many trains, moving at high speeds—usually under tons of concrete and steel, roads and sky-scrapers, surrounded by pipes moving high volumes of water, gas, and electricity—through a series of underground passageways that, in many cases, are more than a hundred years old.

Except when it's a train moving above water on a rickety bridge.

Or when it's a train moving through an old tunnel under a gajil-lion gallons of water.

In other words, the subway system doesn't really need anthrax or bombs to make it a frightening place. The thing is fraught with peril. Considering its age and the way it was abused in the sixties and seventies, that something doesn't go horrifically wrong on a daily basis is one of those minor miracles of urban living—sort of like the fact that falling masonry doesn't kill people more often (which apparently is quite a problem in Edinburgh, Scotland).

As secular and non–God fearing as city dwellers are made out to be, we put a great deal of faith in things. No one ever doubts a traffic light or crossing signal (until it's too late). No one gives more than a second's thought to walking under four-story-tall scaffolding (until you see such a thing come crashing down). No one worries about a brick, due to years of weather extremes, dislodging from a skyscraper and hurtling toward the sidewalk.

This is no doubt done to preserve sanity. After all, if a New Yorker did start considering all the things that could possibly go wrong, he'd never get to work.

But removing the blinders of faith is an interesting thought experiment, and it occurred to me almost a full year before September 11, partly because I've always been a paranoid Doubting Thomas and partly because I once saw a manhole cover take flight.

I'd just started at a new job in Midtown Manhattan on the second floor of an ugly office building. We were all seated at our computers one morning when we heard a loud boom. Our monitors shimmied, indicating a power surge of some sort. In those innocent days, when the greatest villain in New York was Ralph Nader, we did the natural thing: We ran to the window and pressed our faces against the glass to see what we could see. And what we saw (and smelled) was sulfurous, yellow smoke pouring out of an open manhole. Then just as Con-Ed was about to send some of its workers down into the maw, another boom. On the other side of the intersection a manhole cover, a cast iron Frisbee weighing more than one hundred pounds, went sailing fifteen feet into the air and came clanging down onto the street. Luckily, no one was hurt. Then, I assume, most of my colleagues forgot about it. I didn't. For a few days, I was plagued by what-ifs.

And I'll tell you, being plagued by what-ifs is a mild annoyance when you find yourself stalled on a Q train on the Manhattan Bridge. Typically, when a train stalls on the Manhattan Bridge, a sane person takes a few moments to bask in the glory of New York—the grandeur of the Manhattan skyline, the gritty but welcome sight of Brooklyn, the silent majesty of the Brooklyn Bridge. An annoying person will whip out his cell phone and start making calls. But what I was doing was asking myself what if. What if a cable snapped? What if the tracks were rotted through? What if the bridge, I don't know, just broke? I was wondering how far the drop was (135 feet), wondering how old the bridge was (ninety years old), wondering what would happen to a subway car hitting the water from such great heights (I think we can use our imaginations on that one) and, lastly, wondering if the teenager sitting next to me would notice he was about to die or simply continue saying "Fuck yeah, son, you know it" into his cell phone all the way down.

Instead of putting these thoughts out of my head and offering up a prayer to the subway gods when I arrived safely home, I turned to Google. All I will say of my findings is that if you're at all like me, you really should ignore this little Manhattan Bridge fun fact pointed out by the Web site nycroads.com: "Maximum torsion occurs when subway trains start to cross opposite sides of the bridge at the same time. At that moment, one side of the roadway dips four feet to the north side, while the other side of the roadway dips four feet to the south side, creating a total roadway deflection of up to eight feet."

Ooh. Fun! Further: "Even the passage of a single train caused microscopic cracks to develop, and over the course of decades, larger cracks developed."

Of course, the Manhattan Bridge was renovated starting in the mid-80s, and we can rest assured that all those issues were addressed, because nothing says competence, efficiency, and attention to detail like a city bureaucracy.

At least on a bridge, some part of your mind convinces you that somehow, some way, you could survive the fall and then swim for freedom. Such delusions are harder to maintain when sitting on an F train stuck on the tracks in the East River subway tunnel and your mind starts with the questions. What if there was a crack in the tunnel? What if it had been slowly growing for the last sixteen years? How often do they inspect these things? What if a couple million gallons of water came pouring into the tunnel? Would the weight of the water and the collapse of the surrounding walls crush the train and kill me outright? Would that entire river flow in at once and drown me? Or would it pour in at a speed just fast enough to slowly fill the train with mud, slime, and cold water, giving me plenty of time to realize I was going to die? Would the last thing I heard before dying be the screaming of a hysterical woman with big hair, bad mascara, and acrylic fingernails with flower decals?

And this was before I knew anything about the tunnels. Did you know, for instance, that the only thing between you and imminent demise is a security blanket devised in 1914, when they started building the East River tunnels? Seriously. From Consulting Engineer, F. Lavis, in the December 24, 1914, *Engineering News*:

> In several places the roofs of the tunnels are quite close to the river bed, so that additional cover must be provided. Owing to the swiftness of the tidal current at this point and its scouring action, the problem of retaining a clay blanket in place according to the method heretofore used in East River tunneling seemed to be one of some difficulty. The method proposed, however, will not only probably retain the clay, but by placing the material at this time (November, 1914) it will settle well into position and become nearly impervious, by the time the tunnels are driven.

The method unveiled, the day before Christmas in 1914, was the standard clay security blanket made stronger by . . . mud. And rocks.

Merry Christmas, New Yorkers. Your safety depends on the mud dredged up from the Jersey side of the Hudson River. It was believed this would "probably" work. It would be "nearly" impervious. How's that for faith?

For the record, the bottom of the East River tunnel is eighty feet below the surface of the river.

Of course, the sort of mind that dredges up these scenarios always tries to conjure up some miraculous way to escape. What if the force of the water just squirted the train along the tracks and it popped out in Brooklyn? Wouldn't that be fun? It would be almost like a flume ride! Subway surfing would take on a whole new meaning!

But I'm a firm believer that there are limits on good luck. And all the luck the East River tunnels ever had was used up by one Richard Creegan, a worker who helped build the subway tunnel. During construction, a hole formed in the roof and he was sucked up, through the tunnel, through the sand and mud, through the river, and to the surface. Alive.

Tunnel collapse. Bridge falling down. Just two of the many things that could go wrong on the subway on any given day. Believe me, there are plenty more. There are the natural disasters: sink-holes, flash floods and, God forbid, earthquake. There are the man-made ones: muggings, shootings, knifings. And the freak ones: electrical fires, derailments, random CHUD attacks (that's Canni-balistic Humanoid Underground Dwellers for the uninitiated).

Hell, a piece of masonry could fall off of a skyscraper down onto the street below, sending an ice-cream truck careening into a water main, which breaks open, flooding a nest of rats below the streets, which sends them scurrying into the open doors of an express train just before it pulls out of the station, which means ten cars of scream-ing, frantic passengers come tearing out into the Grand Central Ter-minal platform, trampling me to death before I even get on the train.

I can't possibly be the only person who thinks like this from time to time. Certainly, anyone who's lived in the city and possesses any sort of imagination at all has had a fleeting thought or two of subway disaster. But dwelling on this sort of thinking would lead to paralysis. If you thought like this on a daily basis, chances are you'd never be able to leave the house. Chances are you wouldn't make New York City your home. (And if you were that sort of person and had the grave misfortune of being born in New York . . . well, I guess that would explain those people who make newspaper nests in their apartments and live off of deliveries of canned cat food.)

So we, the city dwellers, learn to shut down portions of our minds. We filter, we compartmentalize and put faith in the system (or in something higher than the system). And we ignore. Hell, we already have plenty of practice in that. We ignore the misery of a packed train during a hot, humid rush hour. We ignore the homeless, the winos, the crazies, and the gropers. We ignore all the ghastly scenarios that could play themselves out on any given day, and we go about our lives. Since we do it every day, have been doing it all the while and had planned on doing it for however long we stayed in the city, adding a few more scenarios to that list—suicide bombers, improvised explosive devices, anthrax, ricin—wasn't as hard as we thought it would be. And, to be honest, I think quite a few of us were surprised at how easy it was.

It's not that subway riders are rude or brave or tough or have an attitude (although we certainly do have an attitude). We've simply reached and are able to maintain a transcendent state of subway existence. We've transgressed the shackles of so-called reality and arrived at a state of ignorant bliss.

In other words, we're just callous . . . in the best sense of the word.

Ken Wheaton was born and raised in Opelousas, Louisiana. There, he drove a 1985 Honda CRX. He now calls Brooklyn his home and the 2 train his ride. He writes for Advertising Age *magazine, dabbles in fiction, and wastes hours blogging at http://nondatinglife. blogspot.com.*

Sources:

PBS-TV. "The American Experience: New York Underground." http://www.pbs. org/wgbh/amex/technology/nyunderground/nyundergroundts.html, 1997.

Standing Up

Megan Lyles

My grandfather started driving his brother-in-law's bread truck when he was twelve years old. He's in his eighties now, and he still drives his Grand Marquis around Brooklyn. He'd tried the subway a couple of times, once to take his sister somewhere and once to show my mother how to get to school. Both times he got lost, rode around the system for a while, exited at a random stop, and took a taxi the rest of the way. He has since stuck with his car. Now he doesn't get to Manhattan very often and he knows how expensive it is to park in midtown, so when it came time for my long-awaited college graduation (I was twenty-seven), we took the subway.

It was morning, the tail end of rush hour and crowded, even way out at Fort Hamilton Parkway, even in the last car. Though my grandfather is still fairly spry, he didn't realize how abrupt and forceful the train doors are. They started to close as he was stepping into the train, and I had to brace them open with my body to prevent them from closing on him.

There were no empty seats. We had a fairly long ride ahead of us, and my grandfather looked unsteady on his feet. I was worried about him, and that was new for me. He was fifty-four when I was born; he's always been old to me. But still, our roles had always been clear: He was the adult, and I was the child. He looked after me. He cooked for me when I visited and he carried things that were heavy. He still worked six days a week, running a flower shop with his sister. Of course I helped when I could and he appreciated the gestures, but never really needed them.

Now he was swaying on the W train, his gnarled hand the oldest one grasping the pole. I wanted to circle him with my arms and protect him. Yet no one offered him a seat. I made a visual survey of the people sitting, checking for signs of impending departure. No one seemed to be moving. I looked at my grandfather again. Was it just to me that he looked old? He was dressed for my graduation, and looked very handsome . . . but old. Why didn't anyone stand up for him? I shivered in the aggressive air-conditioning and regretted not hiring a car service.

We passed 9th Avenue, then 36th Street. The crowd swelled and we were shuffled over, but still no seats opened up. And then, finally, someone got up. We were on one of the trains that I always think of as the new trains (though they haven't been new for twenty years), the ones with the orange and yellow seats in L-shaped formations instead of the long, straight rows of benches. The seat that opened up was the inner seat in the short side of the L, the corner seat by the window.

My grandfather smiled at me—smiled up at me, I realized. He was the closest to the seat, so clearly it was his, regardless of age. My grip on the pole relaxed as he prepared to maneuver past the person sitting in the aisle seat.

Then suddenly a woman was shoving past him, practically stepping over him. She was thick and sturdy-looking, not young but definitely not old. My grandfather looked at me again, this time with a kind of resigned shrug. She was going to take the seat and he was going to let her.

I didn't even know what I was going to do until I realized I was squeezing the nubby wool shoulder of the woman's jacket with my right hand. I don't touch strangers. No one does on the subway. At least not under ordinary circumstances. Just as I realized I was touching her, I heard my voice ring out, "Will you let him sit down, please?" Polite enough words, but my tone was anything but. I'm a quiet person. Generally people lean a little closer when I speak, or they focus and try to read my lips. And I can be passive-aggressive. If someone stole my seat, my response would be limited to pointed glares. But this time I spoke—and heads turned. I had made myself heard even above the rattling subway din.

The woman raised her hands in an exaggerated gesture, rolled her eyes and eased back. "OK, OK," she said, as if she had to acquiesce to my ridiculous and unreasonable request only because I was so unstable and potentially violent that, as a sane person, she had no choice. Whatever. She gave up the seat and that was all that mattered. My hand slid off her shoulder. I was shaking a bit, still hearing the echoes of my voice speaking up for the first time in my life.

Too late it registered that my grandfather was protesting. He didn't want me to do it. He didn't want me to say anything. But he sat in the empty seat. Whether to avoid further attention-drawing discussion or because he simply needed to sit, I couldn't tell. He closed his eyes. Was he tired? Embarrassed? I tried to figure it out by looking at his face, at his hands clasped in his lap, but I couldn't tell what he was thinking. I realized I had never seen him on the subway before, with the black void rushing behind his head, yellow lights flashing past. He looked even older with his eyes closed.

I had done the wrong thing. He would rather have stood and suffered and let a lady sit down. Maybe he wasn't finished with the part of his life where he could be gallant to a woman, and perhaps even ask her out to dinner. He liked women slender and polite and giving, not stout and pushy and selfish like this one; still he would have been a gentleman whether she was a lady or not. My hand still tingled with the feeling of the scratchy, wooly fibers of her jacket. I am a woman too, and my reaction to her was based on her actions, not her gender. She was wrong to try to take the seat, and I would have regretted not saying something. I had done the right thing. But somehow I had also done the wrong thing.

And then it turned out to be all for nothing. The graduation venue was empty except for stacks and stacks of chairs. The ceremony we had rushed to get to was not on Tuesday, but Wednesday. We had arrived a day early.

"You're lucky I love you," my grandfather said. I felt forgiven, though we never discussed what happened on the train.

Two subway-less years later I made an appointment to take him to StoryCorps at the World Trade Center. StoryCorps is a project that was developed to record ordinary people's stories. For a nominal donation, you can sit in a soundproof booth with someone and interview him or her. The forty-minute interview is recorded for you on a studio-quality audio CD and, if you sign a release, stored at the Library of Congress. It's a chance to record a little bit of personal history for the future.

It seemed to me like my grandfather had aged more between eighty-two and eighty-four than he had between seventy-five and eighty, and that gave me a sometimes overpowering feeling of "before it's too late." He has always told me stories and I wanted a chance to record some of them, so I could have them forever. And it would be a chance to let him teach me something again, to show him that I still look up to him.

We took the subway again. But this time was different. My grandfather, who had just recently learned to send e-mails, navigated the Metrocard machine and bought his own single-ride card. He stepped easily onto the train before the doors closed, and since we were traveling in the mid-afternoon, we had no trouble getting seats on the way into Manhattan.

He had been surprisingly agreeable to the StoryCorps idea, and the recording session went well. Afterward, he signed the release form and now his stories, about the war, about my grandmother, about his life, are a part of researchable history.

On the way home, we transferred from a half-empty R train to a crowded D train. At first no one moved and I felt that twist of worry again, but then a man got up and pushed my grandfather into his seat, turning away to make it clear there was to be no argument.

At 36th Street, an announcement was made that the M train across the platform would be leaving first, so we ran to transfer. On the M train, a young woman smiled and stood up so my grandfather could sit down. As we pulled out of the station, the conductor announced that the M train would be going express after the next stop, skipping Fort Hamilton Parkway. Ah, the MTA. We got off at 9th Avenue and waited on the muggy platform for the same D train we had just left. Once back on the train, a teenage girl offered her seat, and my grandfather thanked her, but with one stop to go he chose to stand. We stood by the doors and as we clattered above the neighborhood, I showed him how we could see his house, and he showed me where he had rented a room with my grandmother after he came home from the war.

"People are so nice," he said later. "Like the doctor from next door. When he sees me shoveling snow, he comes out to do it for me. He doesn't know I like to do it; he thinks he's helping. And all those people giving me their seats on the train." He shook his head. "I must be old," he said. And he laughed.

Megan Lyles *grew up in Brooklyn near the Fort Hamilton Parkway stop on the B line. She has fond memories of the time when trains were decorated with graffiti and cooled naturally by open windows. Now a travel writer based in Manhattan, she still sometimes stands at the door in the very front of the train to watch the tunnel rush at her, but she manages to resist the temptation to swing around the poles. Visit her Web site at www.meganlyles.com.*

COLLECTING OLD SUBWAY CARS

Lawrence Block

I n 1964 I was living in Tonawanda, a suburb of Buffalo, New York. People who live in suburbs have cars, and I had a 1963 Rambler, and didn't like it much. So one day I drove it to a Volkswagen dealer and made arrangements to trade it in on a new VW convertible. As decisions go, it wasn't a bad one; it was better than the original decision to buy the Rambler, and infinitely superior to the earlier decision to move back to Buffalo from New York.

The salesman and I worked out a deal. I mostly just sat there, not really knowing what the hell I was doing, and this proved to be a good negotiating strategy, as it turned out. Then I filled out the paperwork and signed a lot of things, and arranged to come back in a day or two and give them the Rambler and drive home in the VW.

At which time the salesman kept giving me these strange looks, and I kept waiting for him to say something. And at length he did.

"Tell me," he said. "Where do you keep them?"

"Keep them?"

"The old subway cars," he said. "Where in heaven's name do you keep them?"

If I'd been a computer, I'd have picked that moment to crash. Instead I just stood there, nonplussed, until the penny dropped and I found myself plussed again. And remembered the questionnaire I'd filled out a year or two earlier.

It was in 1961, you see, that my first novel was published—or, more specifically, the first novel published under my own name. It was called *Mona*, and its impact on the world of American letters recalled Don Marquis's observation that publishing a volume of verse was like dropping a rose petal into the Grand Canyon and waiting for the echo. The closest *Mona* got to an echo was the questionnaire that Gale Research, publishers of various reference works including *Contemporary Authors*, sent to anyone who managed to break into print.

It was a fairly straightforward document, and I'd filled it out in a fairly straightforward manner. But then I came to a question about interests and hobbies, and for some reason I turned playful. "Have an extensive collection of old subway cars," I wrote. And, further down the page, I was invited to list topics on which I would welcome correspondence with readers and other authors. "Would like to hear from other collectors of old subway cars," I wrote, "esp. any with wooden cars from the old Myrtle Avenue elevated line."

And then I signed and sealed the thing and mailed it off to Chicago. I didn't really expect them to print it. I mean, really—a collection of old subway cars? And if they did, what could it matter? Who would ever read it?

Well, I'll tell you who read it. That VW salesman read it. I'd told him I was a writer, and so identified myself in the purchase agreement, and he'd decided to check up on me. And he'd found *Contemporary Authors* in the Kenmore Public Library (which, I have to say, was more than I'd ever done, never having thought to look for the listing). And he'd read about my collection and wanted to know more about it.

I've no idea what I told him, but it must have been OK, because I got to drive home in the Volkswagen. (It was the model with the top that you raised and lowered manually. Great little car.)

The car's long gone, but the memory lingers. At the time what astonished me was that the fellow had looked me up, but over time I've decided that what's truly remarkable is that he's the only person in more than forty years to make mention of my putative collection. I've no idea how many copies of *Contemporary Authors* occupy library shelves or how many persons, salesmen and others, may have consulted them. Nor could I begin to guess how many other reference works might have cribbed data from that article. But what I do know is that not a single person has ever raised the subject of old subway cars with me.

It's a damn shame, too. I mean, there has to be somebody out there with a wooden car from the old Myrtle Avenue El. Wouldn't you think?

I love the subway. Always have.

I grew up in Buffalo and came to New York for the first time when I was ten and a half years old. My father, a native New Yorker, brought me for a weekend of male bonding years before someone dreamed up a term for it. We rode the Empire State Limited to Grand Central, stayed next door at the Commodore Hotel, and for three or four days he showed me the city. We went up to the top of the Empire State Building, we took a ferry to the Statue of Liberty, we saw a Broadway show (*Where's Charlie?* with Ray Bolger) and a live telecast (*The Talk of the Town*, the Ed Sullivan show, which was remarkable to me less for the fact that it was live than that it was television; I'd not yet seen TV back home, and found the monitor more interesting than the show onstage). We went all over by subway, and my most vivid memory is of a Sunday morning ride on the Third Avenue El, all the way down to the Bowery. I recall seeing a fellow run out of a saloon down there, let out a blood-curdling shriek, then turn around and run back in again.

It seems to me that I knew then that I'd eventually live in New York. I moved here for the first time in the summer of 1956; I'd just completed my freshman year as an Antioch College student, and the school had (and continues to have) a co-op plan whereby students spend half the year in jobs in their field. My job was as a mail room flunky at Pines Publications, on East Fortieth Street, and I commuted by subway from an apartment on Barrow Street. I would board the 7th Avenue IRT local at Sheridan Square—they call it the 1 train now—and switch to the express at 14th Street and get off at Times Square and walk a couple of blocks.

Curiously, that's always been my train. I've lived in various parts of the city—mostly in Manhattan, but for a while in Greenpoint, Brooklyn—and I've had occasion to ride most of the city's subway lines, but I've always thought of the West Side IRT as my line. Early on, I wrote a song about it, a parody of an old Carter Family classic about a heroic engineer who died at the wheel of a train sabotaged by strikers—one of the rare pieces of folk music written to glorify a scab. Here's the song, which my friend Dave Van Ronk recorded on an early album:

> Along came the IRT, a-cannonballin' through
> From 242nd Street to Flatbush Avenue
> At 5:15 one Friday eve she pulled into Times Square
> The people filled the platform, and Georgie, he was there.
>
> The people filled the platform, they milled and massed around
> And Georgie looked upon that train, and it was Brooklyn bound
> He vowed at once that train to board, the weekend not to roam
> For Georgie was a shipping clerk, and Brooklyn was his home.

The people poured into that train, ten thousand head or more
George used his elbows and his knees until he reached the door
But when he reached those portals, he could not take the gaff
The conductor shut the door on him and cut poor George in half.

The train pulled out of Times Square, the swiftest on the line
It carried poor Georgie's head along and left his body behind
Poor George he died a hero's death, his martyrdom's plain to see
And the very last words that Georgie said were "Screw the IRT."

So when you ride that IRT and you approach Times Square
Incline your head a slight degree and say a silent prayer
For his body lies between the ties amidst the dust and dew
And his head it rides the IRT to Flatbush Avenue.

They don't write songs like that anymore, and it's not hard to see why. Oddly, it had a close brush with success. The Kingston Trio, a very successful pop-folk act at the time, was considering covering it, but recorded their MTA song ("He will ride forever 'neath the streets of Boston; he's the man who never returned") instead. And they decided one subway song was enough.

The West Side IRT, then, was my subway line. And there's something special about one's own subway line.

This became evident in the early nineties, before the crime rate plummeted in New York. The city was then perceived as a dangerous place to be (although even then the perception was probably out of proportion to the reality) and someone sponsored a survey to find out not how safe or unsafe the subway system was, but how safe or unsafe it was thought to be by the hapless souls who rode it.

Most of them, it turned out, gave the system bad marks, allowing that the trains and tunnels were perilous. But the great majority of those surveyed noted an exception—one line in particular, they maintained, was much safer than the rest of the network.

And which line was that? In all the city, which line was the safe one? Why, it was whatever line the passenger in question rode on a regular basis. D train riders felt safe on the D, but kept their guard up on the N. West Side IRTers were nervous when they had to ride the East Side IRT. And so on. Familiarity, it seems, breeds not so much contempt as contentment. We will, if circumstances compel us, take the train less traveled by—but we won't be happy about it.

I've always been puzzled by people who don't take the subway.

Oh, I can understand that out-of-towners might find it daunting. I remember the first time I had to find my way through the system. It was my first summer in New York, and I'd arrived by train from Buffalo and met my roommate-to-be at Grand Central. He told me he'd found us temporary lodgings on West Fourteenth Street and said I should take the shuttle to Times Square and the IRT downtown. Fourteenth was an express stop, he said, so I should take the express, but the local would also get me there. Just as long as I took the IRT, he said, and made sure I was headed downtown.

I hoisted my suitcase and found my way. The Times Square station was swarming with more people than the average American sees in the course of an average day, or even a week, all of them hurrying this way and that with that incomprehensible purposefulness rarely seen outside of an anthill. I didn't pay much attention to them, and they paid no attention to me, and I did what I was supposed to do and emerged at Fourteenth Street and Seventh Avenue with a sense of having accomplished something.

A lot of tourists, I've noted, tackle the subway with the same spirit of adventure and emerge with the same sense of accomplishment. Others take cabs, and I can understand that, although it seems to me they're missing something. But what I find harder to grasp is those New Yorkers who would sooner plunge naked into a sewer than descend into the subway tunnels.

"I haven't taken the subway in over twenty years," a novelist friend informed me. "Thank God and my agent I don't have to."

Success, I guess, means to him that he gets to cram his large body into a small taxi and listen to one side of a cell phone conversation in Urdu while waiting helplessly for the light to change, and change again, and change a third time. The hell, I say, with that.

If it's late and you're exhausted, and if you're trying to get from Eighty-ninth and York to Twenty-third and Tenth, well, yes, there's something to be said for flagging a cab. But in the ordinary course of things the subway is faster and more comfortable. (It's less comfortable at rush hour, but makes up for it in speed. You're a little more miserable, but for considerably less time.)

The only times I've been late for appointments in the past several years have been when I was pressed for time, and reflexively took a taxi in the hope of getting there faster. And, of course, I'd have gotten there sooner by subway. One almost always does.

My characters know this. Most of my books are set in New York, and most of my characters get around the same way I do, dropping a token in the slot (in the earlier books) or swiping a Metrocard.

In *A Walk Among the Tombstones*, a dope dealer in Bay Ridge wants to hire Matthew Scudder to find the men who abducted and dismembered his wife. They don't hit it off, and the man dismisses him and gives him $200 for his time and expenses. Scudder won't take it:

"Take the money. For Christ's sake, the cab had to be twenty-five each way."

"I took the subway."

He stared at me. "You came out here on the subway? Didn't my brother tell you to take a cab? What do you want to save nickels and dimes for, especially when I'm paying for it?"

"Put your money away," I said. "I took the subway because it's simpler and faster. How I get from one place to another is my business, Mr. Khoury, and I run my business the way I want. You don't tell me how to get around town and I won't tell you how to sell crack to schoolchildren, how does that strike you?"

They worked things out, I'm happy to report; otherwise there'd have been no book. And Scudder has continued taking the subway.

In *A Long Line of Dead Men*, he's investigating a string of deaths over a period of several years among the members of a particular club. One is that of a man who jumped, fell, or was pushed in front of an oncoming subway train, and Scudder talks to the transit cop who was the investigating officer, who at the scene's conclusion gives his own take on the subway:

"What I do, I take the subway all the time. I'll be honest with you, I love the subway, I think it's a wonderful and exciting urban rail system. But I am very careful down there. I see a guy who don't look right, I don't let myself be between him and the edge. I got to walk past somebody and it's gonna put me close to the edge of the platform, I wait until I can step past him on the other side. I want to take a chance, I'll go in a deli, buy a lottery ticket. I'll go by OTB, put two bucks on a horse. I love it down in the tunnels, but I don't take chances down there." He shook his head. "Not me. I seen too much."

While I find it hard to understand why any New Yorker would avoid the subway, I'm really puzzled when the person's a writer. One of the many reasons New York is such a splendid city for writers is that one is constantly in contact with one's fellow citizens. In most of the rest of the country, people spend all their in-between time in cars. They listen to their radios or natter away on their cell phones— or, alas, both—and they're effectively insulated from everything going on around them.

If a Los Angeleno's SUV is a culturally sterile environment, a New York subway is a veritable petri dish, swarming with life. Sometimes it's too much; sometimes the peddlers and the mooch artists and the nodding junkies and the militant nonbathers are more than one can bear, and all one wants to do is hide behind a newspaper and tune it all out. But it's life, it's the city, and in a very real sense it's why most of us live here—not for the theater, not for free concerts in the park, but for the urgent pulse of the metropolis.

Overheard in New York is a favorite Web site of mine—and, indeed, of almost everybody I know. It consists of the snippets of conversation submitted by the readers who have in fact overheard them, on the street or in the elevator or, often, in the subway. You don't overhear a lot of interesting things when you're driving around in your car. Overheard in Los Angeles? No, I don't think so.

People ask writers where we get our ideas. It's an annoying question; we get them, mysteriously, from our imaginations, and only someone lacking an imagination would presume to ask the question. But our imaginations, certainly, are stocked by our experience and observation, and we don't enrich them by isolating ourselves.

Writers who don't take the subway? They must be out of their minds.

When I first moved here, I sort of assumed New York's subway was the only one in the world. I didn't think about it much, but whenever another subway was brought to my attention, I was somehow surprised. I'd read no end of French novels with scenes set in the Paris Métro before it dawned on me that the damn thing was a subway.

My wife and I have traveled quite extensively during the past twenty years, and it's been our pleasure to ride the local subway whenever we get the chance. We've taken the Métro in Paris and the Underground in London, naturally, but we've also sampled the subway in Madrid and Barcelona and Stockholm and Rome, in Prague and Budapest, in Minsk and Kiev and Moscow and Tashkent, in Taipei and Singapore . . . and, I'm sure, in other foreign capitals I've temporarily forgotten.

All of these cities have surface-level public transportation as well, but we hardly ever take the bus. When we do, we more often than not get lost. A bus, I've found, cannot be trusted. You think you know where it's going, and then the damn thing takes a turn you didn't expect, and you don't know where the hell you are. You're above ground, you can *see* where you're going, but you're still lost. Underground, where all you can see are the tunnel walls, it's not all that hard to get on the right train and take it to the right destination.

I've noted a few things about various subway systems. I can tell you that the platforms in Paris smell of Gauloise cigarettes, that the tracks in earthquake-prone Tashkent rest upon rubber cushioning, that one line of the Budapest subway is only a few feet below street level, that you risk arrest if you eat or drink anything in the Taipei subway, and that transferring from one line to another in either Madrid or Barcelona involves a longer walk than seems possible. But this is about New York's subway, so all I'll tell you is this: Almost every other system, in this country or abroad, is more modern, more efficient, and more comfortable than ours.

There are, I should point out, some solid exculpatory reasons for this, and chief among them is that we were there first. Our infrastructure is older, and there are no end of things we'd do differently if we'd had the experience of others to build upon.

Remember, too, that New York's subterranean urban transit system began life as three independent subway lines, the IRT, IND, and BMT, each of them authorized by the city but operated by private firms in the wistful hope of profit. That's why, until relatively recently, you couldn't transfer from the E train (IND) to the Lexington line (IRT). The trains crossed one another at 53rd Street, but you had to get out of one, walk a block, and spend another token to board the other. It took decades after the whole business had become a single system before the requisite tunnels were excavated and the two lines fully integrated.

So Paris has maps with little red lightbulbs that show you the best route from one station to another, and London's Underground has genuinely comfortable cushioned seats, and Singapore's trains are—big surprise—as antiseptically clean as Singapore's streets. So what? This is New York. All things considered, we're doing pretty well.

We'd be doing better, I have to say, if they'd built the Second Avenue subway. They started, sometime in the late sixties, and dug up a huge stretch of that thoroughfare, and managed to kill a batch of local retailers and restaurateurs in the process. Then they ran out of money and left things as they were, and sometime in the seventies they gave up and put things back the way they were. (They didn't actually fill in the tunnels they dug, and all that's needed is an appropriation of a few billion dollars and they can start in again where they left off. But don't hold your breath.)

During my first years in New York, I was acquainted with a fellow who was planning a series of stories about a subterranean subculture, a world of runaway children who'd taken up permanent residence in the subway system, rarely if ever emerging on the surface. You didn't have to, he pointed out. You could live on hot dogs and peanuts and Mars bars and Cokes, which was what most kids lived on anyway. You could buy clothes when what you were wearing got too ratty and, if you wanted to look respectable, you could even get your hair cut and your shoes shined. (There's still at least one barber I know of, in the Columbus Circle station, and shops to shine and repair your shoes all over midtown.)

And, as Edmund Love reminded us in *Subways Are for Sleeping*, you could get forty winks and more quite comfortably.

I don't think the stories ever got written. Everybody, as I recall, had something wonderful he or she was going to write, and that's often as far as it went. I myself decided my first novel would be a stirring tale of Ireland's fight for freedom, set in the 1920s. But first, I realized, I really needed to know the whole history of Ireland, and in order to put it in context I'd have to have a thorough grounding in English history. So I went out and bought Oman's six-volume work on Britain before the Norman Conquest. I never got more than a chapter or so into it, and never did write a word of my Irish novel, but I managed to amass an impressive library of English and Irish history. When I wrote my first novel, it turned out to be a story of a young Midwestern woman in Greenwich Village coming to grips with her sexuality, or trying to.

Life, of course, imitates art, even when the art never makes it past the state of conception. A decade or more ago, when homelessness flowered in New York (and, I suppose, elsewhere, but it was always more visible here), our subway system became home to no end of people. The Fourteenth Street pedestrian passageway, running between Sixth and Seventh Avenues, turned into an underground equivalent of the Hooverville shantytowns of the Great Depression. One soon learned not to walk there; it wasn't dangerous, although it may have felt that way, but it was unhygienic in the extreme, and the stench was overpowering.

That's changed now, and the homeless have largely disappeared from the subways, although people still sleep on the trains. Some of them are homeless, and some are heroin addicts on the nod, but others are just drunk, and a few are merely tired. Years ago a good friend of mine, a writer whose name you'd recognize, was tired—well, yes, he'd had a few drinks—and he dozed off on the L train on his way home to Canarsie. When he woke up he discovered that someone had stolen his shoes. These things happen.

It was in 1948 that I first rode the subway, and both it and I are a good deal older now and have had irregular maintenance over the years. I still ride the subway and am in fact the proud possessor of a Senior Metrocard, one of the few tangible benefits of having ascended into Old Farthood.

The card—with my name and picture on it—works just like any other Metrocard, but it gets me onto the subway (or, more rarely, the bus) for half price. And that's terrific, a true perk of age, but it's the least of it.

I never have to refill it. It's linked to my credit card, and it refills automatically. And—get this—every month I receive a statement in the mail, with every occasion I've used the card noted, and the time and place specified. I could, if I cared to, use the thing to find out where I'd been, something I'm less and less likely to recall on my own with the advancing years.

I loved the card from the moment I got it and was heartbroken when I lost it. I figured I'd have to go through a ton of red tape to replace it, and I might even get a scolding before I got a new card. Then I called the designated number, had a five-minute conversation, and a few days later received a replacement card in the mail. I didn't even need to have a new picture taken; they had the old one on file.

Of course! They were dealing with the senescent, a batch of doddering oldsters who needed the card not least of all to remember our own names. Naturally they'd be prepared to deal with lost cards.

The second time I lost my card, I knew just what to do. And I didn't get a scolding that time either.

I wish people wouldn't hold the doors. I wish the public address systems in the stations weren't inaudible. I wish they'd get back to work on the Second Avenue subway. I wish they'd replace those cars they bought from Japan, the ones with the sculpted seats, artfully designed to accommodate a population with smaller behinds. I wish each train had a designated car for passengers who stink to high heaven, so they could all ride together and leave the rest of us alone.

And what I really wish is that I'd hear from other collectors of old subway cars. Hey, if you've got any of those wooden cars from the Myrtle Avenue El, get in touch, you hear? Maybe we can do some swapping. . . .

Lawrence Block's *novels range from the urban noir of Matthew Scudder* (All the Flowers Are Dying) *to the urbane effervescence of Bernie Rhodenbarr* (The Burglar on the Prowl), *while other characters include the globe-trotting insomniac Evan Tanner* (Tanner on Ice) *and the introspective assassin Keller* (Hit List). *He has published articles and short fiction in* American Heritage, Redbook, Playboy, Cosmopolitan, GQ, *and* The New York Times, *and eighty-four of his short stories have been collected in* Enough Rope. *His newest bestsellers are* All the Flowers Are Dying *(February 2005 in hardcover), the sixteenth Matthew Scudder novel, and* The Burglar on the Prowl, *his tenth Bernie Rhodenbarr novel now available in paperback. Larry is a Grand Master of Mystery Writers of America and a past president of both MWA and the Private Eye Writers of America. He has won the Edgar and Shamus Awards four times each and the Japanese Maltese Falcon Award twice, as well as the Nero Wolfe and Philip Marlowe Awards, a Lifetime Achievement Award from the Private Eye Writers of America and, most recently, the Cartier Diamond Dagger for Life Achievement from the Crime Writers Association (UK). Larry and his wife, Lynne, are enthusiastic New Yorkers and relentless world travelers.*

THE FIRST ANNUAL THREE-BOROUGH SUBWAY PARTY

Johnny Temple

There were two clear indications our idea was flawed. The First Annual Three-Borough Subway Party was intended to be an underground fiesta, a choreographed subway routing for a roving band of misfits to transfer through over the course of three hours on a Saturday night. We would bring liquor, marijuana, and fearless wit. The party routing was as follows: Board the 6 train at Astor Place in Manhattan and head up to the Grand Central hub for thirty minutes of loitering, drinking, and random conversation; from there take the 6 train one more stop north to 51st Street and transfer to the E, which would carry us under the East River to Queens Plaza, where we'd catch the much-maligned G train under Newtown Creek (the word "creek" never so blatantly misappropriated) to Bergen Street in Brooklyn; a transfer to the F train would round back to lower Manhattan, and we would deboard at East Broadway and close the party with night-caps at a Chinatown apartment.

The first indication that it wasn't the right time for this particular party was a poster on the wall in the Lafayette C stop near my front door in Fort Greene, Brooklyn. The poster had a hand-drawn police mug shot of a suspect wanted in connection with a brutal crime. Two large black garbage bags filled with body parts had been found in this station on the Manhattan-bound platform.

This was the winter of 1991, before the economic upturn several years later would rid the neighborhood of those tabloid-ready violent crimes that plagued all five boroughs of the city. In 1991, the subway was as good a place as any to rob and beat. Indeed, the entire system seemed to be marinating in a stew of subterranean criminality.

The second overlooked factor in our party planning was the great karmic debt that some of us were racking up with the use of phony subway-token slugs. These were little pieces of metal molded into the shape of subway tokens that worked in the turnstiles just like real ones. My roommate Matt had struck up a friendship with a Chelsea bartender who controlled the slug supply. After Matt's reasonable markup (he was born and raised a Communist Jew, so he wasn't about to gouge us or anything), the rest of us got them for fifty cents each. Our consciences were slightly troubled by this scam—as well they should have been. An adult now (well, actually, I was twenty-five then), I recognize the New York City subway as a miracle of urban planning, of reliable service, of ethnic and economic diversity. The average New York City subway car is an exquisite, rugged reflection of our city's unique character. But I digress.

We were tempting fate with our use of those token slugs. Zeke, one of our party ringleaders, carried an additional karmic debt to the Metropolitan Transit Authority. Several months earlier, when he had been working for a temp agency, Zeke headed out for a job one morning when he discovered that he didn't have any slugs left. Relatively criminal-minded and impudent in those days, Zeke jumped a turnstile at the 2nd Avenue F station and was immediately nabbed by two cops hiding behind a column. Instead of merely issuing a ticket, they cuffed Zeke, along with a gaggle of other fare evaders, and hauled them down to the precinct. Zeke's single permitted phone call went to his temp agency. He got his supervisor on the line.

"Hi Janice, it's Zeke. I'm really sorry, but I'm not at the job. When I got off the subway this morning, I saw a woman get practically run over by a car."

"I'm so sorry to hear that," his supervisor replied.

"It was awful," Zeke elaborated. "She broke her leg—her femur was sticking right out through her thigh. I know CPR, so I tried to help. I rode with her in the ambulance and I'm with her now at the hospital."

"My God, is she OK?" the supervisor gasped.

"I hope so. We don't know yet. It's really awful. But I'm not going to make it to the assignment this morning."

"Oh, don't worry about that. Of course not. I'll get someone to fill in for you. Please don't worry. Just call me back and let me know if she's OK."

The cops laughed when Zeke hung up, then one of them steered him down a hall to a holding area. When Zeke was released from the pen two hours later, he rang his supervisor again.

"Janice, the lady just got out of surgery and it looks like she's going to be fine. She broke her leg and a few fingers, but all her internal organs are OK."

Zeke heard Janice turn away from the phone and call out, "Zeke says the woman is fine!" Cheers rang out through the office and into phone line, settling into an exuberant, "Zeke! Zeke! Zeke!"

For the next several weeks Zeke was awarded the best and most well-paying assignments through the temp agency.

The First Annual Three-Borough Subway Party convened at an apartment that Zeke shared with our friends David and Chris in

Chinatown, on Ludlow Street just north of Canal. My friend John and I arrived early and joined Cristina, Claudia, and the three apartment dwellers in pre-party libations before setting out to the street. Already intoxicated—enough so that the details of this story have been remarkably difficult to establish—we headed toward Astor Place, where we would meet up with a few others and use our slugs to board the 6 train.

As we crossed Delancey along Orchard, a dark brown sedan that had just crossed the Williamsburg Bridge into Manhattan jolted to a stop a few feet away from our legs and honked, causing several of us to lurch back. Inside the car, a group of teens laughed uproariously at the frightened geeks.

Zeke retaliated. While the car full of teens was still rocking with hilarity, Zeke charged right at it and jump-kicked the window—only to swerve away at the last possible moment. Although their vehicle was unscathed, the bridge-and-tunnel crew had stopped laughing. Now it was them who lurched back in surprise.

Suddenly, all four car doors burst open and six big guys piled out, leaving two young women sitting in the backseat, while the car idled in the middle of Delancey. Seeking to avenge Zeke's blow to their collective manhood, these adolescents didn't exactly face formidable opponents in us scrawny hipsters.

Claudia, who is now married to the New Zeke and was part of the roving party that night, recalls how boldly we reacted: "We all split. As fast as we could, in any direction. . . ."

Sorrowfully, she adds, "Except one of us."

Six-sevenths of our group, including Zeke, took off up Orchard Street. My most vivid memory from this night was the acutely cartoonish chase scene in which Zeke, their primary mark, would abruptly cut to the side and the guys after him would slide right on by, then he would dash off in the opposite direction. They'd get back on his tail and Zeke would abruptly stop again, and again they'd skid by. Cristina, who remembers few specifics about this doomed escapade ("I was really drunk"), also has an unusually lucid recollection of what she calls "the horror/comedy" of watching them try to capture Zeke. "There were a whole bunch of them and he was just zigzagging, and they couldn't catch him. It was effortless; he looked like a gazelle." (I appreciate the gazelle imagery, though my own animal simile would be a rabbit—specifically, Bugs Bunny; Zeke likens his own movements to that of a squirrel.)

The predators finally had to give up on their target, since their sedan and the two young women inside were still stranded in the middle of Delancey. Zeke curled off west on Rivington toward me and John.

What impressed me about Zeke's wily escape that night was not his explosive quickness, to which I was accustomed, but his high level of dexterity, even with badly bruised knees. Just a week earlier he had sustained a typically idiosyncratic subway injury. Having moved from temp work to social work (the job transition foreshadowing the arrival of the New Zeke), he was running late for a meeting at a community center in the South Bronx. On the train he realized he was on the 4/5 express instead of the 6 local he should have been on for Cypress Avenue. The express was going to shoot him up to Hunts Point Avenue, where he'd have to turn right around and head back downtown five stops on the local. He'd miss the meeting.

Anxiety snowballing—he needed the income from this job right now—Zeke opened the door and stepped between two subway cars, then climbed up the outer protective grate. The car sped through the Cypress Avenue station, slowing only slightly as it passed Bronx residents waiting for the uptown local. Perched between the two cars, Zeke waited until a column in the station flew by, then leaped. He crashed to his knees and skidded down the platform into an inglorious tumble, somehow avoiding the commuters. Stunned by the bizarro white guy flying off the passing express train, a dozen scattered New Yorkers stood gaping at Zeke, who jumped to his feet and chirped, "Late to work!" It wasn't until he was racing out of the subway station that he noticed what the others had seen—bloody holes in both knees of his dressy black work pants. When Zeke scuttled into his meeting several minutes later, attempting nonchalance, his supervisor gave one look and said, "Zeke, you go ahead and take the day off."

Zeke got away from these six bridge-and-tunnel guys, but David got stomped. An Australian philosophy Ph.D. candidate at the New School University, David had arrived to New York a little over a year earlier as a thoughtful, charming, and wide-eyed young man. After hooking up with our lot, his social habits devolved quickly. But he was still quite pensive—too pensive for this particular situation. When the kids had jumped out of their car and the rest of us bolted, David attempted discretion. "I looked at the ground and made like I was walking past," he tells me over the phone from his home in Melbourne, Australia. "But then I looked up and made eye contact." Immediately a fist clobbered him in the side of the head, knocking off his glasses, hammering him to the ground.

So when the guys who had been chasing Zeke turned back to their car, they spotted, then joined, their buddies, who had surrounded David—now coiled in a protective fetal position—and were giving him a severe boot treatment.

Claudia recalls watching a panicked expression cloud over Zeke's face when he glimpsed the beating under way back at the intersection. From her vantage up Orchard where she had fled with Cristina, Claudia could tell that he thought it was her being pounded into the pavement. There was an intensity and fury to his focus that she had never seen before.

Zeke started to sprint in the direction of the thrashing, then paused and looked back, spotting Claudia and Cristina in the shadows of a bodega awning. He slowed up, massively relieved, gulping air while the hormoniated teens down at the intersection concluded their attack with two final kicks to David's rib cage, then piled in the car and peeled down Delancey.

David uncrumpled on the ground and slowly raised himself to his feet. His glasses were broken and the Pentax camera he had been carrying was gone. Blood was smeared across a wound on his bruised face, and it looked like a clump of his hair had been ripped out.

"Zeke was the instigator and he ended up totally unscathed," Claudia tells me fourteen years later, a hint of mirthful pride betraying her feigned shame.

David didn't go to the doctor, though he appeared to have a mild concussion accompanying his wrenched body. While his physical wounds healed over the next few weeks, the most lasting damage of the incident may have been done to his friendship with Zeke.

Not long after the failed party, David confessed to Chris that he thought Zeke was immoral and that he might even be the Devil. Hard to argue too much with the immoral part—we were all a bit reckless those days, flirting with drugs and other brands of malevolence, Zeke certainly no less than anyone else. But truth be told, it wasn't too long after this party catastrophe that the Old Zeke went into retirement and yielded way to the New Zeke.

So, the First (and Last) Annual Three-Borough Subway Party plunged to a pathetic end that night with nothing gained, and not a single slug slipped into a subway turnstile. But a few things were learned: David learned that his roommate was the living embodiment of the Devil; Zeke, although he did not believe himself to be Satan, had further evidence that he needed to bid farewell to his path of darkness, as it was starting to take its toll on the people around him; Claudia learned that Zeke loved her more deeply than she had ever imagined; and although I remain an avowed agnostic (of the Jewish persuasion), I discovered that I can't escape karmic debts, and neither can I ignore omens such as signs on subway walls about bags filled with chopped-up body parts.

Johnny Temple is the publisher and editor-in-chief of Akashic Books, an award-winning New York–based independent company dedicated to publishing urban literary fiction and political nonfiction. He won the American Association of Publishers 2005 Miriam Bass Award for Creativity in Independent Publishing. Temple plays bass guitar in two bands, Girls Against Boys and New Wet Kojak; both bands have toured extensively across the globe and released numerous albums. Temple has contributed articles and political essays to various publications, including The Nation, Publishers Weekly, AlterNet, Alternative Press, Poets & Writers, and Bust.

Encounter

Jessie Koester

It was a July morning. Not yet nine o'clock and already 90 degrees. I was on my way to work, still half asleep and listless from the heat. The A/C in the subway car was dripping condensation and spitting tepid air. I was irritated: Sticky strangers pressed up against me; sweat trickled down my back; the air felt like wet wool; and still, the woman next to me, facing me, wore a floor-length cloak.

It was thick and lined with a soft fabric, maybe flannel. With the hood pulled up over her head, and the strings tied tightly under her chin, the woman's face was completely shaded. Strands of long, fuzzy brown hair were pulled down through the opening, providing further shield. Her hands were in her pockets, her shoulders hunched, her head hanging on her chest. I wondered who she was hiding from. She was so deeply buried, she didn't seem to notice her hem brushing against my bare ankles.

The subway train veered around a corner and hurtled along a straight stretch of tracks. The screech of the rims on the rails, the sound of metal on metal, made my jaws clench. I closed my eyes to avoid looking at everyone: the old men with wet-through shirt backs, others in suits with briefcases in hand, the bobbing headphoned heads, a woman in nylons, a mother trying to keep her kids from clambering around the greasy pole, a messenger braced against his bicycle, a girl eating an egg sandwich while reading the Bible. Their nearness made me nervous. As the train lurched forward, those of us standing swayed into each other's space. The woman in the cloak lost her bearing and stepped on my foot. She didn't back off. "Excuse me," I said. She didn't respond.

From far away, a horn sounded twice. Then it stopped. And the train stopped too. Without screeching or skidding, it simply shut down, somewhere between the 14th and 23rd Street stations. First, there was a soft thud, then nothing. An almost imperceptible thud, like the shifting of fault lines. Still, I heard it. I felt it go through me. I remembered cornering a bend once—years ago—in my dad's station wagon, at the very moment a deer leaped from the shelter of trees skirting the road. A precise and final moment. The white tree branches swerving and swaying at the side of the road against some invisible force. The deer's eyes wide with shock; its horns mangled in the grill; its legs caught up in the wheel; its body quivering. I remembered sitting on the wet pavement, stroking its hide as the twitching slowed and subsided. In its eyes I saw the empty blue sky curve above us.

When the subway stopped, the lights went out and the air ceased blowing. We were pitched into a dark void. The F train didn't budge, and no one budged within it. We couldn't; we were crammed together. In limbo. The loudspeaker had given up crackling and buzzing. Its muffled, distorted voice had hushed. There were no directions or apologies. But we were relatively calm, buried in the dark, trapped in the heat, far below the bustle of Sixth Avenue. This was well before 9/11.

While the woman stood sheltered in her cloak, the rest of us avoided one another's eyes. We mumbled under our breath and shifted from one leg to the other. We fanned our hands in front of our faces and pulled out our shirttails—our skin glossy with sweat. Our hair went limp. Our shirts stuck to our backs, our skirts and pants to our thighs. The air smelled of eggs and sausage. Coffee. Something sour. We were swelling together. Only the cloaked woman remained apart. There was something about her remoteness that made me picture her at the bottom of a well.

After an hour, some people bent down to sit on the grimy floor. Some started swearing. The "F" train. Some were sleeping. Some were staring at the woman who was covered head to toe. I was afraid she might pass out. If she did, she'd fall on me and, I imagined, I'd fall on the man with the egg and sausage on his breath, and he'd fall on the sour one, and all the way down the line.

Finally a hand appeared from the folds of cloth, fingers clenched, a sliver of gold glinting from her wrist. She jerked on the string and the knot slipped free. When the hood fell to her shoulders, she raised her head as if she were rolling a boulder up a steep incline. The hill was a long one, and halfway up, I wished she'd stop and go back down again. I had a sudden fear she'd reveal too much.

When I was a kid, there was a cave at the top of Rib Mountain. We crawled through a crevice to get inside, where the air was soft and cool and the walls were moist. We picked our way through stalactites hanging from the ceiling and followed the sound of dripping water, down a winding path to the bottom of a wide cavern—the bottom of the world—where we lay down limp and quiet, listening to the murmuring of the earth. In the velvety darkness, I held a hand out in front of my face, and I couldn't see it. The light was just a pinprick above me. I knew it was there, but I closed my eyes to it, and for a while I didn't even miss it.

It's impossible to describe the woman's face, but it was sort of like a collapsed cave. Stalactites of skin hung from the sagging walls and crevices of her neck, nose, chin, and cheeks. They were shaped like piles of prayer rocks, looking ready to topple. The hood hung halfway down her back. She had undone the top buttons at her neck and I could see that her collarbone and shoulders were eroded too. I couldn't imagine how she'd come to be that way. It was like staring at the aftermath of a natural disaster, or a man-made one. Like the damage caused by a landslide, a forest fire, an earthquake, a tsunami, an attempted murder, or a suicide.

The whole time I was trying not to look at her, trying not to jerk away from the hem of her cloak, trying not to burst into nervous laughter, I was oblivious—we all were—to what was going on outside the train. We thought only about how uncomfortable we were in the stifling car, how the presence of the deformed woman made us more so. The two kids had stopped swinging around the pole. They were standing limply, staring at her. "What's wrong with her?" one asked his mother. When she didn't respond, he tugged at her. "What's wrong with her? What's wrong with her? What's wrong with her, Mom?" "What's wrong with *you*?" the mother said finally, "Where are your manners?" That shut him up, although some people looked at the woman in the cloak expectantly then, as if she'd take pity and answer the boy, answer us all. She didn't, of course.

Finally, a swath of light cut through the dimness. A yellow beam swung this way, then that. We shrank back to make room for two men in orange vests who came through the door between cars and walked through our midst. They didn't say a word to us. Their walkie-talkies were buzzing and beeping at their hips. Then they were gone, through the door at the other end of the car.

A while later, a uniformed man with a megaphone and a lantern walked into our car. His face, like those of the other two men, was hard and set. "OK, let's go. Single-file, please," he said. "Walk to the front. Slowly now." He lit the way, and we picked ourselves up and walked one after the other through car after car, until we reached the first car of the train. When it stopped, the subway had just nosed its way out of the opening into the station and the first door of the first car was open to the platform. There was bright light ahead of us, and as we stepped out of the car, we saw a woman pinned down by the train on the tracks below us.

She must have jumped from the platform. Her face was scraped off. She was half-reclining, slick with blood, twisted at the waist, her legs caught up in the underside of the train. A paramedic sat in the sludge between tracks, holding her, bracing her shoulders, and talking to her gently. "You're OK," he said. "You're OK." Two other paramedics and a transit worker stood in a semicircle around them, in an attempt to shield her from view, but between their fidgeting arms and legs, we caught glimpses. Phantom trains on neighboring tracks screamed by without pause. In their wake, all was quiet. The paramedic pressed numbers into a cell phone, and then held the receiver to the woman's ear. She was saying her good-byes before the train was pulled off her, and her insides would fall out. That's how they do it, I know now. I heard her say, "Hello, it's me," and then faintly laugh, as if at the awkwardness of it all. She was in shock.

We walked slowly, single-file down the platform, up the stairs, ushered through the turnstile by the men with walkie talkies and orange vests. The woman in the cloak slid through quickly. I followed her lead. Outside, the heat was crushing. The block was barricaded. Sirens were wailing, red lights flashing from ambulances, fire trucks, and police cars. Without looking back, the woman in the cloak went her way and I went mine. With every step, the sun grew more intense. It was surprising how bright it was. I'd forgotten.

Jessie Koester is the director of Information Services at Poets & Writers. She has an MFA from The New School and recently received a fellowship from Yaddo, where she worked toward completing her first novel.

TUNNEL STORIES

Jennifer Toth

If I had it to do over again, I decided after my last tunnel adventure, I wouldn't. Even after the good reviews and positive publicity for *The Mole People*, after the vindication of having proved what most New Yorkers already knew—that people really do live in the tunnels under New York City—I wouldn't do

it again. I couldn't. It was too difficult. Within five years after the book was published, most of those I knew and visited in the tunnels were dead. Some died from AIDS, a few from TB, a couple from common colds, but most died without anyone caring enough to know the specific cause. Their bodies were simply dragged or carried out of the tunnels and burned. Their lives, like their deaths, evaporated, disappearing from conversation with a heavy, careless shrug and an airy look beyond. Even among themselves, their deaths were always expected.

And that hurt most. I thought I had failed them. I failed to bring the mole people alive to the world. I believed I could change their underground, make it less forbidding and hopeless, by making the tunnels real to the "topside world," as the mole people called it. Perhaps I've let that expectation go so I can remember more of the dark wonder of the tunnels now. Perhaps not, and that's why I still feel a sense of failure and sadness, a loss of part of myself to a wasted darkness.

Almost fifteen years have passed since I wrote my final chapter. New York's underground still follows me. In Marrakech and Berlin, London and Paris, almost without realizing it, I look for people in the dark hollows of tunnels and subways. Whatever city or country, it is the same search. Cupping my hands to the darkened windows at the ends of subway cars, peering down grates, I look for evidence of life. Sometimes I see people wandering the tracks or camped at their sides, and I imagine their stories from the way they walk or sit or stand. Abused child, runaway teen, disturbed war veteran, drug addict, alcoholic, mentally ill, depressed, bipolar, schizophrenic.

I don't tell my four-year-old son the tunnel stories. But he watches me, and he's curious. Without knowing, I've trained him to look for mole people too.

"People live down here?" he asks.

"Sometimes," I say.

"Why?"

"Because they've lost their place in the world up top."

"Why?"

"I don't know."

"Are they sad?"

"We'd probably say so, but they might not think so."

"Are they ghosts?"

"Sort of."

"Are there monsters down here?"

"Sometimes."

I remember then the fragments of stories, the ones that never concluded, the ones that did not make it into the book because I couldn't verify what I'd heard or track down an individual to complete his tale. Those are the stories that keep me wondering, the puzzle pieces that float around in my head.

Today I think of a man who has amnesia. From a car accident, he thinks. When he woke from a coma, he had several grown children, a few grandchildren, and a kind wife of thirty-five years. He could not recognize them. He could remember complicated math equations. He knew how to read. He recited long poems to me, and even longer passages from books I only later read. But he could not remember his family. This did not bother him much at first, but it troubled his family greatly. His personality had changed. He once had an edge to him, they said, a hot temper. At dinner he had held court on everything from politics to art. There was no room for compromise or for other people's opinions. After the accident, he was quiet. When asked, he found he had no opinions whatsoever. He just didn't see the point of opinions. Now he was sweet, and this saddened them—the loss of the person they knew.

"They didn't want to know me as I am now. Every day they mourned for someone I didn't know and couldn't care less about," he said, his face edged with annoyance. "But I was a constant reminder of *him*. One look at me, and my so-called daughter burst into tears." They used their memories like needles, trying to provoke him or at least remind him of who he was.

He had to leave, he said. He had to disappear from the life he had left when his head hit the windshield. He was free now, he claimed, though sometimes he missed his soft bed, a full fridge, and the warmth of a body next to him. But at least he was free of pain, he told me.

He follows me, like many others. Mostly when I don't expect him, he emerges in my mind, when I see one of the new homeless of Berlin with the same shuffle, the same vacant eyes. They are fewer but growing, not as experienced in the ways of the streets and tunnels as New York's more seasoned homeless population. They're still learning, feeling their way, beginning to explore their tunnels. Their faces are paler and more faded, less weather-worn, but I believe their stories are much the same.

Sometimes I think I can remember every minute I spent in the tunnels. I remember the excitement of the adventure, wondering what the next corner held, what the next story told. I can still taste and feel the warm, stagnant air, smell cooking rat, see soot-covered tomato vines planted carefully under a grate to catch the sun. I hear the echoes of people "talking" through a code of pipe taps. Eyes watching me through the dark. Trains coming before their sound, felt in the rails' vibration, seen in the scurrying roaches. Every inch of me alert and alive, terrified but thrilled.

Fifteen years ago, the tunnels held a certain truth for me, a frightening introduction to the real world in all its baseness and hope. I can remember and mourn people who died violent deaths more peacefully now. Those who survived, who kept striving to survive, still fascinate me. Each puzzle piece, even the ones that do not fit and perhaps never will, feels unwasted, as though they carry some clue, some greater understanding I may find along my way.

I'm not certain how or when New York's tunnels turned from ugly and foreboding in my early memory to fantastic and enriching now. But they have. Perhaps my own pain has since then hardened me to the dark memory of theirs. I feel almost possessive of New York's underground now. I lost innocence down there. I look into my son's fresh eyes and in their reflection, I recognize that many of my fearsome and melancholy tunnel ventures have weathered me. Still, I would not give up the wonder of truth and even the beauty of the underground in all its complexity. That is my secret. But perhaps there are some mysteries left in me, some unfilled niches in my mind I don't want answered by dark tunnels, anywhere. I learned so much winding my way through the underground labyrinth, perhaps too much. I don't really need to know that rats prefer doughnuts to bagels with jam, that they're dead smart, and that they're used to seek out bodies because their senses are so keen for a meal. From the safety of the topside world I can still hope that rats are far more mean and fearless in the face of desperation than I would ever be.

Jennifer Toth is the author of The Mole People: Life in the Tunnels Beneath New York City *(Chicago Review Press, 1993),* Orphans of the Living: Stories of America's Children in Foster Care *(Simon & Schuster, 1997), and* What Happened to Johnnie Jordan? The Story of a Child Turning Violent *(The Free Press, 2002). She is currently living in Berlin with her husband, Craig Whitlock—a reporter for* The Washington Post—*and her son, Kyle.*

SPEAK, HOYT-SCHERMERHORN

Jonathan Lethem

Here's where I am: in the subway, but not on a train. I'm standing on one platform, gazing at another. Moaning trains roll in, obscuring my view; I wait for them to pass. The far platform, the one I'm inspecting, isn't lit. The tiles along the abandoned platform's wall are stained—I mean, more than in some ordinary way—and the stairwells are caged and locked, top and bottom. Nothing's happening there, and it's happening round the clock.

I've been haunting this place lately, the Hoyt-Schermerhorn station. But the more time I spend, the further it reels from my grasp. And, increasingly, I'm drawing looks from other passengers on the platforms and upstairs, at the station's mezzanine level. Subway stations—the platforms and stairwells and tunnels, the passages themselves— are sites of deep and walled invisibility. Even the geekiest transit buffs adore the trains, not the stations. By lingering here, I've set off miniature alarms in nearby minds, including my own. I've allied myself with the malingerers not on their way to somewhere else. My investigation of this place reeks of a futility so deep it shades toward horror.

Undercover transit policemen are trained to watch for "loopers"—that is, riders who switch from one train car to the next at each stop. Loopers are understood to be likely pickpockets, worthy of suspicion. Even before that, though, loopers are guilty of using the subway *wrong*. In truth, every subway rider is an undercover officer in a precinct house of the mind, noticing and cataloguing outré and dissident behavior in his fellows even while cultivating the outward indifference for which New Yorkers are famous, above and below ground. It may only be safe to play at not noticing others because our noticing senses are sharpened to trigger-readiness. Jittery subway shooter Bernhard Goetz once ran for mayor. He may not have been electable, but he had a constituency.

As it happens, I'm also an inveterate looper, though I do it less these days. I'll still sometimes loop to place myself at the right exit stairwell, to save steps if I'm running late. I've looped on the 7 train out to Shea Stadium, searching for a friend headed for the same ballgame. More than anything, though, I looped as a teenager, on night trains, looping as prey would, to skirt trouble. I relate this form of looping to other subterranean habits I learned as a terrified child. For instance, a tic of boarding—I'll stand at one spot until a train stops, then abruptly veer left- or right-ward, to enter a car other than the one for which I might have appeared to be waiting. This to shake pursuers, of course. Similarly, a nighttime trick of exiting at lonely subway stations: at arrival I'll stay in my seat until the doors have stood open for a few seconds, then dash from the train. In these tricks my teenager self learned to cash in a small portion of the invisibility that is not only each subway rider's presumed right but his duty to other passengers, whose irritation and panic rises at each sign of oddness, in exchange for tiny likelihoods of increased safety.

By this law of meticulously observed abnormalities, then, my spying here at Hoyt-Schermerhorn goes noticed, triggers a flutter of disapproval in other inhabitants of the station. This may be deserved. I'm not here for a train. I've come seeking something other than a subway ride. What I'm trying to do maybe can't be done: inhabit and understand the Hoyt-Schermerhorn station as a place. Worse, I'm trying to remember it, to restore it to its home in *time*. There's no greater perversity, since a subway station is a sinkhole of destroyed and thwarted time. By standing here trying to remember Hoyt-Schermerhorn I've only triggered its profoundest resistance: I'm using it wrong.

The origins of New York's underground trains, like those of the city itself, reflect a bastard convergence of utopian longing and squalid practicality—land grabs, sweetheart deals, lined pockets. The city's first, thwarted subway was no different: a Jules Verne dream, one instantly snuffed by Tammany Hall, that paradigmatic political machine. The story has the beauty of a Greek myth: a short length of pneumatic subway built in 1869 *in secret* beneath Broadway by a gentleman engineer determined to alleviate the choking daylight nightmare of New York's foot, pig, horse, stagecoach, and surface railway traffic, against the status quo wishes of Tammany's Boss Tweed, who rolled in troughs of money extorted from trolley and omnibus companies. The tube's builder, Alfred Ely Beach, ought to be the hero of one of those elegiac novels of Time Travelers in Olde New York—editor of *Scientific American*, architect of American patent law, he was also a health nut and an opera buff, and the man in whose office Edison first demonstrated the phonograph ("Good morning, sir. . . . How do you like the talking box?"). In fifty-eight nights of covert digging Beach's crew created a 312-foot tunnel, then assembled an elegant wooden, horseshoe-shaped subway car, powered by a giant electric fan. When he unveiled his miracle to the press—in an underground waiting room fitted with curtains, stuffed chairs, painted frescoes, a goldfish fountain and waterfall, grandfather clock, and zircon lamps—his demonstration subway caused a sensation. Tweed, aghast at what had hatched beneath his feet, roused an entrepreneurial assault on Beach's tunnel, investing his capital—and New York's immediate future—in elevated lines rather than subways. The life was squeezed from Beach's dream. His tunnel was rented for wine storage, then forgotten. When in 1912 diggers excavating for the BMT line stumbled unwittingly into Beach's intact waiting room, his drained fountain and extinguished lamps, his stilled wooden car, they must have felt like intruders on Tut's tomb.

When you're a child, everything local is famous. On that principle, Hoyt-Schermerhorn was the most famous subway station in the world. It was the first I knew, and it took years for me to disentangle my primal fascination with its status as a functional ruin, an indifferent home to clockwork chaos, from the fact that it was, in objective measure, an anomalous place. Personal impressions—family stories, and my own—and neighborhood lore swirled in my exaggerated regard. In fact the place was cool and weird beyond my obsession's parameters, cooler and weirder than most subway stations anyway.

My neighborhood, as I knew it in the 1970s, was an awkwardly gentrifying residential zone. The Hoyt-Schermerhorn station stood at the border of the vibrant mercantile chaos of Fulton Street—once the borough's poshest shopping and theater boulevard, it had suffered a steep decline, through the fifties and sixties, from Manhattanesque grandeur to ghetto pedestrian mall. Now no less vital in its way, the place was full of chain outlets and sidewalk vendors, many selling African licorice-root chews and "Muslim" incense and oils alongside discount socks and hats and mittens. The station itself gave testimony to the lost commercial greatness of the area. Like some Manhattan subway stops, though fewer and fewer every year, it housed businesses on its mezzanine level: a magazine shop, a shoeshine stand, a bakery. Most telling and shrouded at once were the series of ruined shop-display windows that lined the long corridor from the Bond Street entrance. Elegant blue-and-yellow tile work labeled them with an enormous "L"—standing for what, exactly? The ruined dressmakers' dummies and empty display stands behind the cracked glass weren't saying.

The station was synonymous with crime. A neighborhood legend held that Hoyt-Schermerhorn consistently ranked highest in arrests in the whole transit system. Hoyt and Bond streets made vents from the Fulton Mall area, where purse snatchers and street dealers were likely to flee and be cornered. The station also houses one of the borough's three transit police substations, a headquarters for subway cops which legislates over a third of Brooklyn's subway system—so perhaps it was merely that suspects nabbed elsewhere in the system are brought there to register their actual arrest? I've never been able to corroborate the legend. The presence of cops and robbers in the same place has a kind of chicken-and-egg quality. Or should it be considered as a Heisenbergian "observer" problem: Do we arrest you because we see you? Would we arrest you as much elsewhere if we were there?

However ridiculous it may seem, it is true that within sight of that police substation my father, his arms laden with luggage for a flight out of JFK, had his pocket picked while waiting on line for a token. And the pay phone in the station was widely understood to have drug-dealers-only status. Maybe it does still. For my own part, I was once detained, not arrested, trying to breeze the wrong way through an exit gate, flashing an imaginary bus pass at the token agent, on my way to high school. A cop gave me a ticket and turned me around to go home and get money for a token. I tried to engage my cop in sophistry: How could I be ticketed for a crime that had been prevented? Shouldn't he let me through to ride the train if I were paying the price for my misdeed? No cigar.

Other peculiarities helped Hoyt-Schermerhorn colonize my dream. The station featured not only the lively express A train, and its pokey local equivalent, the CC, but also the erratic and desultory

GG, a train running a lonely trail through Bedford-Stuyvesant into Queens. The GG—now shortened to the G—was the only subway line in the entire system never to penetrate Manhattan. All roads lead to Rome, but not the GG. Hoyt-Schermerhorn also hosted a quickly abandoned early-eighties transit experiment, "The Train to the Plane"—basically an A train which, for an additional fare, ran an express shot to the airport. For my friends and me the Train to the Plane was richly comic on several grounds—first of all, because it didn't actually go to the airport: you took a bus from the end of the line. Second, for its twee and hectoring local television ad—"Take the train to the plane, take the train to the plane," etc. And last because the sight of it, rumbling nearly empty into Hoyt-Schermerhorn with the emblem of an airplane in place of its identifying number or letter, suggested a subway train that was fantasizing itself some other, less inglorious and earthbound conveyance.

The Train to the Plane was younger cousin to a more successful freak train, also run through Hoyt-Schermerhorn: the Aqueduct Special, which took horse-racing bettors out to the track on gambling afternoons. It flourished from 1959 to 1981, when it became a casualty of Off-Track Betting, the walk-in storefront gambling establishments that soon dotted the city. The Aqueduct Special made use of Hoyt-Schermerhorn's strangest feature: its two quiescent tracks and dark spare platform, that parallel ghost—the platform I'd come to gaze at so many years later. As a kid, I took that dark platform for granted. Later, I'd learn how rare it was—though the system contains whole ghost stations and vast graffiti masterpieces, no other active station has a ghost platform.

Even if I'd known it, I wasn't then curious enough to consider how those two unused tracks and that eerie platform spoke, as did the ruined display windows, of the zone's dwindled splendor, its former place as a hub. Where I lived was self-evidently marginal to Manhattan—who cared that it was once something grander? What got me excited about Hoyt-Schermerhorn's fourth platform was this: one summer day in 1979 I found a film crew working there, swirling in and out of the station from rows of trucks parked along Schermerhorn Street. Actors costumed as both gang members and as high school students dressed for prom night worked in a stilled train. The movie, I learned from a bored assistant director standing with a walkie-talkie at one of the subway entrances, was called *The Warriors*. My squalid home turf had been redeemed as picturesque. New Yorkers mostly take film crews for granted as an irritant part of the self-congratulatory burden of living in the World Capital. But I was like a hick in my delight at Hoyt-Schermerhorn's moment in the sun. I was only afraid that like a vampire or ghost, the station wouldn't actually be able to be captured in depiction: What were the odds this crappy-looking movie with no movie stars would ever be released? By picking my turf the crew had likely sealed their doom.

I became a regular customer in 1978. That year I began commuting most of the length of Manhattan, a one-hour ride from Brooklyn to 135th Street, to attend Music and Art, a famous public high school. The A train out of Hoyt-Schermerhorn was now my twice-daily passage, to and from. My companion was Lynn Nottage, a kid from the block I grew up on, a street friend. Lynn was from a middle-class black family; I was from a bohemian white one. We had never gone to school together in Brooklyn—Lynn had been at private school—but now were high school freshmen together, in distant Harlem. Lynn had the challenge of getting to school on time with me as her albatross. Some mornings the sound of her ringing the doorbell was my alarm clock.

We were students not only of Music and Art but of the A train. Our block felt in many ways like an island in a sea of strife, and Hoyt-Schermerhorn was a place where the sea lapped at the island. Lynn and I had a favorite bum who resided in the station's long passage from the Bond Street entrance, whom Lynn called "Micro-Man," not for his size but for the way his growling complaints boomed in the echo chamber of the station like a microphone. One day Lynn screamed theatrically: she'd spotted a rat behind the smeared glass of the mezzanine-bakery's display counter. I quit buying doughnuts there. Downstairs, we'd fit ourselves into jammed cars, child commuters invisible to the horde. The trip took an hour each way, long enough going in for me to copy the entirety of Lynn's math homework and still read four or five chapters of a paperback. (I'd read another third or so of each day's book at school, during lunch hour or behind my desk during class, then finish it just as we pulled into Hoyt-Schermerhorn again on the return trip. By this system I read five novels a week for the four years of high school.)

Lynn and I had habits. We stood in a certain spot on the platform to board the same train every morning (despite an appearance of chaos, the system is regular). Most mornings we rode the same subway car—the conductor's car. Had we been advised to do this by protective parents? I don't know. Anyhow, we became spies, on the adults, the office workers, tourists, beggars, and policemen, who'd share segments of our endless trip. We took a special delight in witnessing the bewilderment of riders trapped after Fifty-ninth Street, thinking they'd boarded a local, faces sagging in defeat as the train skipped every station up to 125th, the longest express hop in the system. Also, we spied on our own conductor. The conductor's wife rode in with him to work—she'd been aboard since somewhere before Hoyt-Schermerhorn—then kissed him goodbye at a stop in the financial district. Two stops later, his girlfriend boarded the train. They'd kiss and moon between stops until she reached her destination. Lynn and I took special pleasure in witnessing this openly, staring like evil Walter Keane kids so the conductor felt the knife-edge of our complicity. Twenty-five years later I'm haunted by that wife.

This was the year another student, a talented violinist, had been pushed from a train platform, her arm severed and reattached. The incident unnerved us to the extent we were able to maintain it as conscious knowledge, which we couldn't and didn't. There were paltry but somehow effective brackets of irony around our sense of the city's dangers. Lynn and I were soon joined by Jeremy and Adam, other kids from Dean Street, and we all four persistently found crime and chaos amusing. The same incidents that drew hand-wringing from our parents and righteous indignation from the tabloids struck us as merry evidence of the fatuousness of grown-ups. Naturally the world sucked, naturally the authorities blinked. Anything was possible. Graffiti was maybe an art form, certainly a definitive statement as to who had actually grasped the nature of reality as well as the workings of the reeling system around you: not adults, but the kids just a year or three older than you, who were scary but legendary. The entire city was like the school in the Ramones' movie *Rock 'n' Roll High School*, or the college in *Animal House*—the dean corrupt and blind, the campus an unpatrolled playground. Our own fear, paradoxically, was more evidence, like the graffiti and the conductor's affair, of the reckless, wide-open nature of this world. It may have appeared from the outside that Lynn and Jeremy and Adam and I were cowering in this lawless place, but in our minds we romped.

The names of the three limbs of the subway—the IRT (Interborough Rapid Transit), the BMT (Brooklyn-Manhattan Transit), and the IND (Independent Subway)—are slowly falling from New Yorkers' common tongue, and the last enamel signs citing the old names will soon be pried off. Slipping into shadow with those names is the tripartite origin of the subway, the fact that each of the three was once a separate and rival corporation. The lines tried to squeeze one another out of business, even as they vied with now-extinct rival forms: streetcars and elevated trains. On this subject, the language of the now-unified system, the official maps and names, has grown mute. But the grammar of the lines and stations themselves, with their overlaps and redundancies, their strange omissions and improvised passageways, still pronounces this history everywhere.

The early subway pioneered in crafty partnership with realtors and developers. Groping for new ridership, owners threw track deep into farmland, anticipating (and creating) neighborhoods like Bensonhurst and Jackson Heights. But the IND, which built and operated Hoyt-Schermerhorn, was a latecomer, an interloper. Unlike its older siblings, the IND clung to population zones, working to siphon excess riders from overloaded lines. The city's destiny wasn't horizontal now, but vertical, perhaps fractal, a break with the American frontier impulse in favor of something more dense and strange.

The new trains running through Hoyt-Schermerhorn quickly mothballed both the Schermerhorn trolley and the old Fulton elevated line—but first the station had to be dug. Construction of new stations in a city webbed with infrastructure was a routine marvel: according to Stan Fischler's *Uptown, Downtown,* tunneling for the IND required, beyond the 22 million cubic yards of rock and earth displaced, and 7 million man-days of labor, the *relocation* of 26 miles of water and gas pipes, 350 miles of electrical wire, and 18 miles of sewage pipes. What's notable in period photographs, though, is the blithe disinterest in the faces of passersby, even at scenes of workers tunneling beneath a street where both a trolley and an el remain in operation. The Sixth Avenue tunnel at Thirty-fourth Street was an engineering marvel in its day, a dig threaded beneath the Broadway BMT subway and over the Pennsylvania Railroad (now Amtrak) tubes, as well as an even-more-deeply buried water main. "The most difficult piece of subway construction ever attempted," is almost impossible to keep in mind on an F train as it slides blandly under Herald Square today.

Alfred Kazin, in *A Walker in the City,* wrote:

> All those first stations in Brooklyn—Clark, Borough Hall, Hoyt, Nevins, the junction of the East and West side express lines—told me only that I was on the last leg home, though there was always a stirring of my heart at Hoyt, where the grimy subway platform was suddenly enlivened by Abraham and Straus's windows of ladies' wear . . .

When a friend directed me to this passage, thinking he'd solved the mystery of those deserted shop windows in the Hoyt-Schermerhorn passage, I at least had a clue. I searched the corporate history of Abraham and Straus—Brooklyn's dominant department store and a polestar in my childhood constellation of the borough's tarnished majesty, with its brass fixtures and uniformed elevator operators, and the eighth floor's mysterious stamp- and coin-collector's counters. In the A&S annals I found the name of a Fulton Street rival: Frederick Loeser and Company, one of the nation's largest department stores for almost a century, eventually gobbled up by A&S in a merger. The 1950s were to such stores as the Mesozoic was to the dinosaurs—between 1952 and 1957 New York lost the Loeser's, Namm's, Wanamaker's, McCreery's, and Hearn's; the names alone are concrete poetry.

I'd nailed my tile-work "L": Loeser's created display windows in the new Hoyt-Schermerhorn station to vie with A&S's famous (at least to Alfred Kazin) windows at Hoyt. Kazin's windows are visible as bricked-in tile window frames today, but like the smashed and dusty Loeser's windows of my childhood, they go ignored. Meanwhile, aboveground on Fulton Street, the name Loeser's has reemerged like an Etch A Sketch filigree on some second-story brickwork, as lost urban names sometimes do.

The abandoned platform was a mystery shallower to penetrate than Loeser's "L." The extra track connects the abandoned platform to an abandoned station, three blocks away on Court Street. This spur of misguided development was put out of its misery in 1946, and sat unused until the early sixties, when the MTA realized it had an ideal facility for renting to film and television crews. The empty station and the curve of track running to the host platform at Hoyt-Schermerhorn allowed filmmakers to pull trains in and out of two picturesque stations along a nice curved wall, without disturbing regular operations. The non-pareil among the hundreds of movies made on subway property is the subway-hijacking thriller *The*

Taking of Pelham One Two Three. It was in Hoyt-Schermerhorn's tunnel that Robert Shaw and his cohorts stripped off fake mustaches and trench coats and, clutching bags of ransom millions, made their hopeless dash for daylight, and it was in Hoyt-Schermerhorn's tunnel that Shaw, cornered by crusading MTA inspector Walter Matthau, stepped on the third rail and met his doom.

And then there's *The Warriors*. The film is based on a novel by Sol Yurick, itself based on Xenophon's *Anabasis*, an account of a band of Greek mercenaries fighting their way home through enemy turf. Yurick translated Xenophon into New York street gangs; his book is a late and rather lofty entry, steeped in the tone of Camus's *The Stranger*, in the "teen panic" novels of the fifties and sixties. Next, Walter Hill, a director whose paradigm is the Western, turned Yurick's crisp, relentless book into the definitive image of a New York ruled by territorial gangs, each decorated absurdly and ruling their outposts absolutely.

The movie inspired a wave of theater-lobby riots during its theatrical run. It's a cult object now, lauded in hip-hop by Puff Daddy and the Wu-Tang Clan, and cherished by New Yorkers my age, we who preen in our old fears—call us the '77 Blackout Vintage—for mythologizing the crime-ruled New York of the seventies more poignantly, and absurdly, than *Kojak* or *The French Connection*. For, in the film, it is the gang themselves who become the ultimate victims of the city's chaos. In this New York, even the Warriors wish they'd stayed home. For me, a fifteen-year-old dogging the steps of the crew as they filmed, it was only perfect that a fake gang had occupied Hoyt-Schermerhorn's fake platform. The film, etching my own image of the city into legend, began to work even before its public life.

Yurick's book has been reissued again, with a *Warriors* still on the jacket and a long new author's Introduction, detailing the classical and existentialist roots of the novel. Yurick shares his perplexity that this least ambitious of his books should survive on the back of a movie: "There hasn't been one film made in the United States that

I would consider seeing five times, as many who love the film version of *The Warriors* did." Years later, I met with the wizened Yurick on a train platform, though not the subway. We disembarked together in Providence, Rhode Island, each a guest at the same literary conference, and, unknowingly, companion riders on an Amtrak from New York. Our hosts had failed to meet our train, and as the locals all scattered to their cars, the family members or lovers to their reunions, we were left to discover one another, and our dilemma. Yurick shrugged fatalistically—should we have expected better? He summed his perspective in a sole world-weary suggestion: "Wanna nosh?"

Michael Lesy's 1973 book, *Wisconsin Death Trip*, is a mosaic of vintage photographs and newspaper accounts of eccentric behavior and spastic violence in turn-of-the-century rural Wisconsin. In a flood of miniature evidence it makes the case that stirring just under the skin of this historical site is mayhem, sexuality, the possibility of despair. The book, a corrective to homilies of a pastoral American countryside, is a catalogue of unaccountable indigenous lust, grief, revenge, and sudden joy.

Poring over old newspaper clippings that mentioned the station, I began to imagine my equivalent to Lesy's book: *Hoyt-Schermerhorn Death Trip*. "TWO ARE KILLED BY POLICE IN GUN BATTLE, 1/23/73: Neither of the slain men was immediately identified. But the police said that one of them had been wanted for several bank robberies and for allegedly shooting at policemen last Wednesday night in the Hoyt-Schermerhorn Street subway station . . ." "WOMAN HURT IN SUBWAY FALL, 6/19/58: A 55-year-old woman was critically injured yesterday when she fell or jumped in front of a southbound IND express train at the Hoyt-Schermerhorn Street station in Brooklyn . . ." "37 HURT IN CRASH OF TWO IND TRAINS, ONE RAMS REAR OF ANOTHER IN DOWNTOWN BROOKLYN DURING EVENING RUSH, 7/18/70: . . . there was a rending of metal at the crash, she said, and then the car tilted. All the lights went out. She said there were sparks and the car filled with smoke. The girl said she was thrown to the floor and, terrified, began screaming..." "STRANGER PUSHES WOMAN TO DEATH UNDER A TRAIN, 2/2/75: A 25-year-old woman was thrown to her death in front of an onrushing subway train in Brooklyn yesterday by a man who apparently was a total stranger to her, the police said ... the incident took place at about 6:15 p.m. in the Hoyt-Schermerhorn IND station, which was crowded with shoppers at this time. According to witnesses, including the motorman, the man suddenly stepped up to the victim, who had her back to him, and pushed her forward in front of the train without saying a word..." "400 BOYCOTTING STUDENTS RIOT, HURL BRICKS, BEAT OTHER YOUTHS, 2/18/65: Four hundred boycotting Negro students broke through police barricades outside Board of Education headquarters in Brooklyn yesterday in a brick-throwing, window-breaking riot ... The disturbances spread over a two-mile area and onto subway trains and stations ... A group of 60 youths attacked a group of six white students on the Clinton-IND's GG line ... They were apprehended at the Hoyt-Schermerhorn station by 15 transit policemen..." "300 IN SUBWAY HELP TILT CAR AND RELEASE BOY'S WEDGED FOOT, 9/2/70: A rescue team of subway passengers, hastily organized by three transit policemen, tipped back a 54-ton subway car last night to free an 11-year-old boy whose foot was wedged between the car and the platform at a downtown Brooklyn station ... The boy ... was running for an IND A train when his leg was caught between the platform and train at the Hoyt-Schermerhorn station."

Contemplation of the life of a site like Hoyt-Schermerhorn becomes, in the end, tidal. The lapping of human moments forms a pulse or current, like the lapping of trains through the underground tunnels, or like the Doppler-effect fading of the certain memories from the planet, as they're recalled for the penultimate time, and then the last: When will the last person to have purchased panty hose or a razor at Loeser's or Namm's pass from the earth? When will the last of those three hundred who rocked the train car off the boy's pinned leg, or the last of those four hundred Negro boycotters, be gone?

A white kid raised inside the liberal sentiments of a middle-class family yet living in an area fringed with crime and poverty met a choice. It was possible to identify with and assimilate to the harsher truths of the street, and so toughen, somewhat, to fear. Alternately, a kid could carry his parents' sensitivities, and standards, with him, out-of-doors. The price was obvious. Most of us, whether we ended in one camp or another, wavered. I was a "good" kid, and a bullied one, yet I recall dozens of moments when I slid briefly across the separation line. Once, on a basketball court, I allowed myself to meld into a crowd of Puerto Rican kids, with whom I'd been playing, as they briefly halted the game to harass and threaten a single Asian man, a gay man, off a neighboring court. I wasn't violent; the incident hardly was. But the man was the boyfriend of a pal of my mother's and I'd been a guest in their elegant town house. When my mother's friend, a gay man considerably huskier than his young lover, returned to the court with a baseball bat and, bellowing, sent us scurrying from our game, his eyes met mine and I was disgraced, wrenched between concurrent selves.

The moment was precursor to a worse one. This was the summer between high school and college, which is to say the verge of my escape from Brooklyn for the first time. I've come to understand how fraught that moment was for me, as I considered or refused to consider what I was involuntarily carrying with me out of my childhood environment. My girlfriend was from upstate New York, but lived in my city, my neighborhood, for that summer before we both embarked to college. She worked nights as a waitress in Manhattan and rode the A train in and out of Hoyt-Schermerhorn. She was frightened, as she perhaps should have been, to walk the several blocks home from that station after eleven, and so I'd promised always to meet her. I often lightly mocked her fear—but that bit of overcompensation, lousy as it sounds, wasn't my crime.

My crime was this: one night, going to the station to pick her up, I impulsively waited in shadow by the entrance instead of making myself visible. I had no plan. I was fooling around. She paused and looked for me, just for a moment, plainly afraid to stand there waiting alone, as she absolutely should have been: it was a different thing to walk swiftly home than it was to linger. I could have stepped forward easily, but instead, frozen in my stupid jape, I only watched her. And then, as she began walking home without me, I followed.

I was certain she'd turn and see me, and that it would be oddly funny, but she never did. She was afraid to turn to see whose footsteps followed her, of course. I trailed her home, compounding my mistake with each accelerating footstep, until I at last overtook her just outside the door. While I tried to explain, she trembled, in fear which converted immediately, and rightly, to rage. Denial has covered any recollection of my words by now, but I know they were hopelessly inadequate to repair what I'd told myself was a harmless joke—though I was walking behind her I'd still been protecting her, hadn't I?—and was actually such a cruel joke it wasn't a joke at all. I'd hardly claim to be Patty Hearst, but there was a touch of the Stockholm syndrome in my behavior. I was bestowing on another a trace, or more than a trace, of the fear I'd absorbed for years.

The glamour of Abraham and Straus, for so long the one survivor among Brooklyn's great stores, has evaporated. A&S's carcass houses a Macy's now, with a small plaque on its Hoyt Street side commemorating the history of A&S, if you want to seek it out. Me, I don't have the heart to go inside the Macy's to see what remains of A&S's Art Deco elevators—let it remain the place where I first met Santa, where I used to buy wheat-backed pennies to fill holes in my penny collection, and thousand-piece jigsaw puzzles.

Not that those memories would likely be diminished by a visit. Perhaps, instead, I'm afraid of their intensification. Every time I pass through Hoyt-Schermerhorn's Bond Street corridor, past

Loeser's tile "L" and bricked-up windows, I recall the first time I saw them, and the start of my lifelong romance, a New Yorker's typical romance with our limitless secret neighborhood, the one running beneath all the others. This was my first subway memory, here: the passage, those windows. Nothing subsequent, not thousands of high-school days, not *The Warriors* nor my own feeble crimes, can displace this memory's primacy, or fade its color. I held my mother's hand. I was being taken to her office, in Manhattan. Perhaps it was a day off from school, I don't know. I rode the subway for the first time I can recall, but I don't remember the train. I remember the station.

Jonathan Lethem is the author of six novels, including The Fortress of Solitude *and* Motherless Brooklyn, *which won the National Book Critics Circle Award. He is also the author of two short-story collections,* Men and Cartoons *and* The Wall of the Sky, the Wall of the Eye, *and is the editor of* The Vintage Book of Amnesia. *His essays have appeared in* The New Yorker, Rolling Stone, Granta, *and* Harper's. *He was the recipient of a MacArthur Fellowship in 2005. He lives in Brooklyn and Maine.*

From *The Disappointment Artist* by Jonathan Lethem, copyright © 2005 by Jonathan Lethem. Used by permission of Doubleday, a division of Random House, Inc.

A BEAUTIFUL BOY

Vivian Gornick

The train was pulling into the 14th Street station as I—late for an appointment at 59th Street—ran down the stairs. Just ahead of me on the platform was a young man (T-shirt, jeans, crew cut) with an elaborately folded-up baby carriage on his back, leading a very small child—three or four, I'd say—by the hand. As the doors opened, he headed for the seats directly ahead of us. I plopped down on the one opposite him, took out my book and reading glasses and, settling myself, was vaguely aware of the man removing the carriage from his back and turning toward the seated child. Then I looked up. The little boy was the most grotesquely deformed child I had ever seen. He had the face of a gargoyle—mouth twisted to the side, one eye higher than the other—inside a huge, misshapen head that reminded me of the Elephant Man. Bound around the child's neck was a narrow piece of white cloth, in the center of which sat a short, fat tube that seemed to be inserted into his throat. In another instant I realized that he was also deaf. This last because the man immediately began signing. At first, the boy merely watched the man's moving fingers, but soon he began responding with motions of his own. Then, as the man's fingers moved more and more rapidly, the boy's quickened, and within minutes both sets of fingers were matched in speed and complexity.

Embarrassed at first to be watching these two so steadily, I kept turning away, but they were so clearly oblivious to everyone around them that I couldn't resist looking up repeatedly from my book. And then something amazing happened: the man's face was suffused with such delight and affection as the boy's responses grew ever more animated—the twisted little mouth grinning, the unaligned eyes brightening—that the child himself began to look transformed to me. As the stations went by, and the conversation between the man and the boy grew ever more absorbing to them, fingers flying, both nodding and laughing, I found myself thinking, "These two are humanizing each other at a very high level."

By the time we got to 59th Street the boy looked beautiful to me, and the man beatific.

Vivian Gornick writes memoirs, essays, and literary criticism. Among her books are Fierce Attachments, The End of the Novel of Love, *and* The Situation and the Story. *Her newest book is a biographical essay:* The Solitude of Self: Thinking About Elizabeth Cady Stanton. *She lives in New York City.*

WHAT'S THE GOOD WORD?

Calvin Trillin

Not long ago, the people in my neighborhood—Greenwich Village, in lower Manhattan—were faced with a new problem. Our subway stop was being made beautiful, and we hadn't figured out how to complain about it. The phrases that trip most easily off the tongues of New Yorkers are expressions of complaint. If a linguistic anthropologist camped out in Manhattan for a while, I suspect he'd discover that New Yorkers have fifty or sixty different phrases for expressing irritation and maybe two for expressing enthusiastic approval ("not that bad" and "it could be worse").

The average subway rider would associate expressions of enthusiasm with people he'd describe as being from "Iowa or Idaho or one of them." (As I have pointed out before, true New Yorkers do not distinguish among states that begin with the letter "I.") For generations—since long before the great cities of this country became associated in the public mind with their problems rather than their wonders—New Yorkers have believed in the old saying that they learn at their mother's knee: "If you can't say something nice, you're never in danger of being taken for an out-of-towner."

This was not the first time the Metropolitan Transit Authority had presented us with an awkward situation: in recent years, all the old subway trains in New York have been replaced with shiny new silver trains, which are absolutely free of graffiti. They are also air-conditioned.

If you live outside of New York—or if you are one of those thick-headed New Yorkers who prefer traffic jams to subway travel—you are probably thinking that the preceding paragraph was one of my little jokes. It wasn't. The New York subways really do have flashy new cars, but New Yorkers rarely mention that fact. It's a difficult thing to complain about.

Not impossible. I've heard a lot of people complain that the absolutely frigid air-conditioning in the subway cars makes the stations, which are still not air-conditioned, seem even hotter than they are. I've heard people say that they miss the graffiti—which is apparently cleaned off at the end of every run, so that there isn't much reason to put it on in the first place—and resent the censoring of this urban folk art by the philistines who run the MTA. It is also possible to complain about how the decision to acquire new cars was made—or, to put it in the local vernacular, how the MTA unilaterally and high-handedly, without consulting the people who actually use the subways every day, decided to force comfortable and attractive new subway cars on the public.

Improvements in the transportation system rarely meet with the approval of New Yorkers. Some years ago, the then mayor, Edward I. Koch, came back from China smitten with the idea of bicycle transportation. He had protective strips of concrete installed to create a bicycle lane up Sixth Avenue. People complained. Eventually, the concrete strips were removed.

I mentioned at the time that you might have expected the taxi-drivers to hate the Mayor's innovation, since it had cost them basically one lane of traffic. ("He likes China so much, he shoulda stood in China.") But who complained the most bitterly about the bike lanes? The bicyclers. The true New York bicyclers—particularly the messengers—complained that the bike lane was full of pedestrians and garment-center pushcarts and bike riders who were described as "schlepping around on Raleigh three-speeds."

"Schlepping" is Yiddish, a language that all true New Yorkers—including Irish cops and Dominican grocers and Pakistani news dealers—speak a little of, partly because its rhythms are famously conducive to complaint. One Yiddish word that all New Yorkers are familiar with is "kvetch"—which actually means "to complain." You often hear them say to each other, "quit kvetching"—to no apparent effect.

So you can see the sort of problem my neighbors and I faced as workmen in our station replaced worn tiles and restored lovely old mosaics. At first, we made do with complaining about the pace of the work. ("Are they ever going to finish this place?") A couple of people tried to argue that the stunning new floor would be slipperier than the grungy old floor.

At one point, while a neighbor and I waited for an uptown local, I decided that I had to express my approval of the renovations, even at the risk of being taken for somebody from Indiana or Illinois. (I'm from Missouri.) "Not that bad," I said, gesturing toward the shiny tiles and the stunning new floor.

My neighbor looked around. "It could be worse," he admitted. "But where the hell is the train?"

Calvin Trillin has been writing for The New Yorker *for more than thirty years. His many books include* Tepper Isn't Going Out, Travels with Alice, Remembering Denny, Family Man, The Tummy Trilogy, Deadline Poet, *and* Too Soon to Tell.

"What's the Good Word?" Copyright © 1995 by Calvin Trillin. Originally appeared in *The New Yorker*. Reprinted with permission of Lescher & Lescher, Ltd. All rights reserved.

WHAT I FEARED

Elise Juska

In 1984 I was eleven and scared of everything. I was visiting my cousins in Park Slope and riding the subway for the first time. My real house was outside Philadelphia, where the sum total of my experience with public transportation was the school bus, one plane ride, and the car pool to CCD.

We'd gone uptown to the Cloisters museum, which I recall as a sensation of space and darkness, nervousness, a giant staircase, and my cousin Kenan distributing Pez. He called them "power pills" as he snapped the jaws of the plastic dispenser. I thought they looked like medicine and made my jaw sting too, though I clung to the faint hope that they might empower me for the ride back downtown.

The subway on the way up had been nerve-wracking but empty, or empty enough that I could keep my fears in check. But the ride going back was a different kind of animal: oppressive, too warm and too crowded, a mash of unwanted intimacies, armpits and sweat stains and strangers so close you could see the hairs on their knuckles, the pores on their chins. My cousin Kieran, also eleven but far more worldly, tried to reassure me. But I clutched at a center pole, eyes glued to the door and tears streaming down my cheeks.

Back in Park Slope, I made it halfway up the first-floor staircase before throwing up. I was not a kid who threw up, so on the rare occasions I did, it felt dramatic and unsettling—underscored in this case by it happening in Aunt Mary Ann's and Uncle Billy's house, a four-story brownstone and, to me, a veritable museum in itself. Their stairs seemed impossibly high and wide, grand and gleaming, Cloisteresque, and the bathroom glowed at the top like an island of pretty soaps and soft white light.

Afterward, I was tucked under an afghan in front of the TV, sipping ginger ale and watching golf. I'd never watched golf before but was instantly won over: the slow pace, the commentators' soothing voices, the comforting names of players like Ernie Els and Fuzzy Zoeller, the endless acres of green outdoors. In short: it was the opposite of the subway, which I was never riding again.

Things that scared me in 1984: escalators, elevators, parking garages, elevators in parking garages, the tiny elevator in the Empire State Building, the *Great Glass Elevator*, locked doors, beggars, the Soviet Union, downtown Philadelphia, dogs, fire, kidnappers, gas stoves, apartment buildings, nuclear war, the library scene in *Ghostbusters*, the man dressed like a pirate who sat in our local Roy Rogers, God, camping, kissing, New York City, the *Dif'frent Strokes* abduction episode, the *Webster* hotel room fire episode, all drug lingo learned in health class (hash, horse, H, pixie dust), airplanes, matches, the dark, the afterlife, the *Jaws* ride at Universal Studios, unwrapped Halloween candy, outer space, the Body of Christ, and my sister's Snuffleupagus doll with the insane plastic eyeballs and tufted brows that glared at me in the dark like a killer in disguise.

So my fear of the subway was not surprising, but it instantly earned the distinction of number one on my list. It contained several essential fear ingredients: not only a confined space but a confined space underground in New York, which was like a space within a space within a space. Toss in the screeching of metal, the occasional splashes of darkness, the skin and sweat of strangers. And most of all, the doors which, every time they closed, contained the possibility that they wouldn't open.

* * *

By 1984 I had been trapped twice, literally. Once when I was eight, at my father's college reunion at St. Joe's, when another alumni daughter and I ventured to the bathroom and got locked in a stairwell. I didn't know this girl, but I thought that we would die together. We grabbed each other and cried, banging on the tiny window—in hindsight it is the size of a porthole, the lawn the size of a football field—at the specks that were our parents picnicking in the distance.

Two years before, when I was six, my cousin Maureen and I had gotten trapped in my great-grandmother's bedroom in North Philly. In the thick, cloying summer heat, the old wooden door had finally swollen shut. We sobbed as we pictured our family— mothers and fathers, aunts and uncles, Grammy and Poppop and Little Nana—downstairs munching chips, listening to the sounds of the new Bruce Springsteen album that drifted upstairs from the record player. We would die alone and they were listening to Bruce: the final twist of the knife.

It didn't occur to us that our parents wouldn't leave without us, that eventually someone would hear our cries. The world had shrunk to the size of that room.

Doors were a cornerstone of my childhood fears, though the nature of the fear depended on the nature of the door. In public I feared closed doors, afraid they would get stuck and keep me from leaving. I watched the entire musical *Annie* looking over my shoulder at the Exit sign, while nearby little orphans sang and danced with rich people.

At my house, I feared the door would be unable to keep strangers out—or us in. My parents demonstrated over and over the inner workings of the front lock: the pebbled, penny-colored surface, the three holes like a hard spiral binder, the deadbolt sliding up, down, up, down, reassuring me that no one could come inside. The deadbolt also felt like proof my parents weren't planning to abandon me, a fear for which I had no sound basis, except that I loved my parents and feared everything. In bed, I would strain to hear the sound of the screen door cringing open, picture my parents tiptoeing across the porch. If they were too silent too long, I would sneak down—unnoticed, I thought—to the landing, where I could peek at their reflections in the living room mirror.

Ultimately, it took only my father sitting on the foot of my bed and saying "We're not going to leave you" for the worry to disappear. This easy disposability was typical of how I dealt with fears in general, like a kind of physical maneuvering: circumvent, destroy, avoid. In a haunted house, when invisible hands grabbed my bare ankles—the fingers were damp, soft, Twinkies with nails—I was ushered out an emergency exit and remained inconsolable while actors in ghoulish masks smiled and joked in attempts to prove they were real people.

Frequently, while typing stories up in my room, I would come flying downstairs and pause on the landing. "What's wrong?" my parents asked.

"I scared myself writing," I said.

Sometimes the fears were disposed of literally, like the Sesame Street album, the one with the scary song about Snuffleupagus searching for his ancestors. I heard this song once and couldn't sleep. It didn't matter that it wasn't playing, it was alive downstairs, lurking in the record itself, sliding like oil through the grooves.

In the middle of the night, my mother had me sit down on the floor in the upstairs hallway. I watched as she broke the record into pieces. "See?" she said, cracking it in half. It was thrilling, empowering, seeing what wasn't supposed to be broken break. "Now it's gone," she said, and had me throw the pieces in the trash can, insisted I be the one to do it, to feel the fear leaving my hands.

I felt secure growing up, which I suppose is a different thing from safe. I was secure in my family's love for me, not just my parents but my entire dad's side—fiercely affectionate pockets of Juskas scattered throughout the Northeast—and my mom's, a close umbrella of relatives at home in Philly who gathered for constant birthdays, holidays, sacraments, underscored by the cracked bats and swelling cheers of the games on TV, surrounded by familiar foods like macaroni salad and pink fluff. My aunts—Kathleen, Mare, Margaret, Jeanne—were a murmur of empathy around a dining room table, exchanging other people's sad stories—neighbors, in-laws, people in their parishes—while my uncles—George, Jack, Tom, Jim, Bill—were a forest of arms reaching out to tickle us as we ran by the TV.

On the first day of sixth grade, when my gym-turned-health teacher told us, "Soon you'll hit a stage where you'll stop wanting to be around your family," I hated her instantly, thinking: *I will never feel like that.*

Because I loved my family, deeply and absolutely, so much so that I was terrified at the thought of them ever changing. At the center of that love/fear was my own living room: nighttime, homework done, freshly showered and pj's on, Mom in the rocking chair and Dad working the "caterpillar comb" through my wet hair. Our house was kind, cozy, airtight inside and out. And yet, there was an undertone of alertness. Of caution, watchfulness. I was growing acutely aware of a larger, less fortunate, more dangerous world that existed beyond my own—a world encompassing everything from Ethiopia, where children were starving, to Northeast Philadelphia, where, that spring, Uncle Bill had cancer. Uncle Bill was a cop and had danced the jitterbug on *American Bandstand*. He was dying, though I didn't understand this at the time. I knew that Mom spent most nights at his house, that my sister and I ate a lot of Ellio's pizza, and that "Uncle Bill is very sick," which is what Mom told me, once, in the car, sitting at the stop sign at the bottom of our street. We lived at the top of a hill, and climbed up it painstakingly slowly, Buick groaning under the weight of all that steepness and sadness.

At home, my parents prepared us for any emergency: reviewed our fire alarm procedure, stashed a ladder under their bed and stuck silhouettes of firemen to my sister's and my bedroom windows. This sense of vigilance extended to just about everything: bedtimes, curfews, money, manners, feelings, health. When the Olympic volleyball player Flo Hyman died of Marfan's Syndrome, my parents saw I had some of the same (tall, long-limbed) symptoms and took me and the Marfan's article from *Newsweek* to Children's Hospital. After an echo and EKG, it was determined I did not have Marfan's, but did have a common heart condition called mitral valve prolapse. The sound my heart made was a "squish," the doctor told me, using his thick, dry, freckled fingers to model the tricky way my valve moved, inside out, like a flipper on a pinball machine, a miniature door in my heart.

Would it be too easy a conclusion, my fear of being trapped ultimately trapping me? It feels too obvious, as plotted as the story of when I was a newborn and our house was broken into, a story I knew so well growing up it took on the sheen of an urban fairy tale. I knew the kitschy part, the album cover with Elton John in big white sunglasses that was forever empty because the record had been on the turntable the robbers stole. I knew the funny part, that the robbers had rifled through Mom's jewelry but left it all because there was nothing valuable enough to take. I knew the moral, to always leave some lights on even if thunderstorms were in the forecast. I knew the sweet, triumphant ending, where the round wooden box that held my baby money fell off the TV as they were stealing it, rolled across the floor, and stayed closed.

I knew the literal part too: the long slice the robbers had cut in our back door screen. It had been patched securely but the evidence remained, alarming in its bluntness and immediacy. Throughout my childhood I would picture the robber's hand prying through that wire and trace my finger along the cut, like a scar. When we went on vacation, Mom told us to picture our house surrounded by blue to keep it safe. Years later I learned that, for weeks after the robbery, my then-twenty-seven-year-old father slept on the couch, keeping watch.

* * *

What I feared had a quality of inevitability. I had watched enough local news to believe that being shot in one's lifetime was more than likely. It had happened to Ronald Reagan and the pope. It happened in Philadelphia every day. I began concocting contingency plans for terrible things that might happen to me.

Plan A: If homeless and starving, go to Roy Rogers. Order the cheapest thing on the menu that could require a fixin'—usually the basic hamburger, wrapped in suspiciously damp silver foil—then clean out the entire fixins bar, piling lettuce and pickles into napkins and making for the exit. I felt guilty about this scheme but reasoned I would be leaving the tomatoes, because I hated them, and would have paid for the burger, so technically I was entitled to it. (My attempts at street smarts were hindered by my weekly doses of Catholic education starring Sin, Punishment, and my teacher Mr. Tucci, all of which scared me more than being homeless.)

Plan B: If attacked on the street, act crazy. Talk nonsense. If performed well, I was sure I could scare the attacker much more than they'd scared me. I was paralyzingly shy, but somehow imagined that in such a moment I could rise up out of myself, compelled by fury, by necessity, and all my latent inner turmoil and hidden emotion would overtake me to save my life.

* * *

My ability to be streetwise had no basis in reality. This was never more apparent than when I spent time with my Brooklyn cousins;

to me, the definition of urban cool. Theirs was the first house I knew with a security system. They had a NO RADIO sign propped in the window of their Saab (the implications terrifying, the strategy ingenious). Their fearlessness was emotional, too. I once overheard my older cousin Kristin read an entire short story she loved to her friend on the phone, which seemed the kind of intimate, literate friendship teenage girls in New York must have. Around Kieran, I was tongue-tied while she confided in me about complicated friendships with boys in Brooklyn, boys who had last names for first names, who exchanged moody, meaningful mix tapes and had relationships that seemed as fraught as adults'.

To her credit, Kieran tried to make me braver. She made me call a boy I liked, pretending to have forgotten the homework assignment. She put mascara on me for the first time saying, "You should start wearing this. You look like Ally Sheedy."

But Kristin was the epitome of daring: she rode the subway to high school. To me, this was an unfathomable combination. At our grandparents' house in New Jersey, she showed off her new, short haircut with long bangs.

"My subway defense," she said, demonstrating how with a toss of her head the bangs fell in a single, shiny swoop over her eyes, and people laughed like it was cute and clever.

My own plan for the New York subway was still intact: avoid, at all costs, forever.

At night, I prayed.

I prayed because I feared the repercussions of not praying. I prayed because I was afraid of my CCD teacher, because I was haunted by the embroidered sampler that hung in the little white bedroom at Nana and Poppy's: *And if I die before I wake, I pray thee Lord my soul to take.* I was also afraid (naturally) of what might be hiding under my bed (mummy, robber, pirate from Roy Rogers) and couldn't bring myself to kneel beside it. So I compromised by kneeling on the bed itself, setting into motion a fresh round of worries (that God would think my kneeling lazy, like the able-bodied people in church who leaned their butts against the pews, or think my prayers—let me do well on this test, let me be kissed by a boy, any boy, in my lifetime, ever—superficial). I prayed for all of my relatives by name, for Uncle Bill in Heaven, and for the children starving in Africa.

Then I crawled on my knees to my window and leaned my elbows on the sill, chin on hands. I liked this pose; it made me feel like a forlorn girl in a movie gazing out her window, a moment prime for poignant voiceover. In the movie she would be wishing on a star, but from my window stars were rarely visible. What light I could see beyond the foggy ink blots of the streetlamps were the headlights and brake lights of a distant highway, beyond which I knew was the border of North Philly, and the apartment building where my friend Marcia was told not to open her door for white men, and the supermarket where the carts were shackled together with chains. But I wasn't focused on any of these; I was watching my secret city.

The secret city was a blinking red light; a radio tower, I would later learn, but at the time I imagined it a faraway civilization no one knew about but me. It was the opposite of the world I lived in—bright, quick, vivid, filled with people scurrying like worker ants throughout the night. Although up close I feared that kind of motion, from behind my flame-colored TotFinder decal I was mesmerized by its distant, steady red pulse. It was a city made miniature, rendered harmless, reduced to the size of a fingernail in my window while I watched from the other side.

* * *

I went to college in Maine, nine hours away from home. I was prepared with everything on the recommended freshman checklist, most of it courtesy of a one-stop shopping trip for wool and flannel at L.L. Bean. I missed my family, wrote them letters, put my little cousins' school pictures around my dorm rooms. Fall of my junior year, when Poppop died the morning the Phillies lost the World Series, I went home for the funeral and my family gathered, as we always did, tearfully joking that it must have been Poppop listening to the games on the radio that had kept our team alive.

That summer, Uncle George was diagnosed with esophageal cancer. The night before his surgery, we converged at Aunt Kathleen's. The next time we saw Uncle George, he would be coming out of a coma, his voice thin, throat patched with stomach lining. But for now, we did what we did best. My uncles vacuumed out the backyard pool, my aunts filled the kitchen with heaps of lunchmeat, fruit salad, pink fluff. At the end of the night, we grabbed up the sleepy babies, our hugs and kisses clinging to Uncle George an extra, noisy second.

My decision to resume a relationship with the New York subway, like many decisions about relationships in New York, was driven not so much by conviction of emotion but financial necessity. After college I found myself there frequently visiting friends, though I couldn't admit to them how much I dreaded riding. It was still an almost physical aversion—not the doors specifically, but the feeling of being trapped and hurtling into darkness panicked me just the same.

I rode selectively, trying to avoid the subway alone, or at night, and if it couldn't be helped, chose cars with people who looked harmless. If I found myself in a near-empty car with someone who made me nervous, I got off at the next stop.

My fear wasn't detectable—just the opposite. Ironically, all my years of shy self-protectiveness had wrought, in the eyes of the world, a thick skin. I discovered that, much as I had always feared New York, my fearfulness helped me fit in there. Walking along Broadway, I fell in step with the city, moving quickly, looking busy, boot heels snapping against the pavement. I did not smile, did not look approachable. I was as wary and distrustful as anybody else. Maybe in New York, I thought, many people were driven by this same impulse: to move quickly, stay aboveground.

But it was underground, on the subway, that my assimilation

was complete. My lifelong nemesis had become my unexpected ally. Here was a place where to be hard and hidden was permissible, even reasonable. Where, even when it doesn't seem possible anyone has ever had such intimate knowledge of that stranger's naked wrist, your eyes are allowed to slide vacantly over his and his over yours. Where, even if your mouth turns down naturally at the corners—prompting strangers above ground to shout, "Let's see a smile!"—on the subway it doesn't make you unfriendly. It's just good sense.

Uncle George had been in remission for two years when the doctors discovered cancer in his liver. Nine months later, they took extreme measures to keep him alive for the birth of his third child. Three weeks after that, the doctors said there was nothing more they could do, he had anywhere from two days to two weeks. He died the next day.

"Daddy went to Heaven last night," Aunt Margaret told my cousin Gina.

She was seven. "But where is he?"

"He's in Heaven, honey."

"No," she said, determinedly. "Where *is* he?"

Aunt Margaret looked at her. "He's at the funeral home."

What scares me as an adult: the unknown, the things you can't see coming, the things that can befall the family you love. It's the red light pulsing on an answering machine on a Saturday in March that you know means Uncle George has died, that is your mother's voice telling you to call her in the same calm, broken voice she once used to describe suffering on the other side of the world. It's standing in front of your classroom aware of nothing but how fragile life is, watching your students who are not so much younger than you are, noting their movements—a pencil scratching, sneaker tapping—proof that they are all still alive. It's the call at midnight on a Monday that is your sister saying she needs help, she's throwing up fifteen, twenty times a day. Or on a Wednesday afternoon, just when you are finally beginning to feel like a grown-up goddamnit, when your parents tell you, "We've been having some problems" and suddenly all those years of cautious silence come rushing into the light. It is no longer one sad thing, it is many sad things; it is the possibility of sad things. You long for records and haunted houses, fears breakable into little parts. But you are not a child anymore; even if the fear is out of sight, you know it's there.

Uncle George's wake was on a cold night in March. My Brooklyn relatives came and Uncle Billy said he'd never seen a line so long; it extended several blocks, past the 7-Eleven that people were ducking into for coffee and hot chocolate. The next morning, after the funeral, Gina stood alone outside the church. I remembered myself as a little girl, strategizing how to protect myself if attacked, all that latent emotion I was counting on to save me. I hadn't been so wrong, I thought; the attack just wasn't what I was expecting. I watched Gina watch my uncles and father and cousin carry the coffin, slide it into the back of the hearse. But where *is* he? One hand was touching her face, the toe of one patent leather shoe turning slowly on the sidewalk.

* * *

It was in my late twenties, riding the subway, that I began looking up. Riding was part of my routine by then, too much so to actively dread it, though I still felt pangs of the old anxiety now and then. In crowded cars, I was detached as anyone, letting my eyes graze that man's shoulder or elbow or top of that woman's head. But on a certain kind of ride—half-empty, caught in a long pause between stops on an express—I watched the people.

In those moments, it felt like the city was drawing a breath, like a cut between takes. The rush and flux of the streets was held fixed, just briefly, and in that pause everything trapped inside rose to the top. Looking around, I watched the blur sharpen into specifics: the man by the door with a scarred lip and thick walkman ears; the young woman, legs twined like a newel post, hair that was perfect this morning but had slipped from its barrettes; the mother with the baby on her lap, chin resting on top of his head but eyes somewhere else; the teenage boy with head sleeping against his girlfriend's shoulder, his eyes closed, hers open.

After Uncle George died, Mom started going to church every morning. The same church where Uncle George was buried, the same church I grew up in fearing God. She carved out a time to sit with it, she said, to seek comfort, "to touch the sadness." I didn't understand this at the time, but in New York, on the subway and away from my family, the ritual began to make a tentative kind of sense. Maybe it had less to do with being in the church than with the people inside it. You don't know them, but look closely and you'll recognize them—the ankle turning in a pair of nylons, the hands clutched in a lap, the deep, sad lines around a mouth.

Elise Juska grew up outside Philadelphia and received her master's in fiction writing from the University of New Hampshire in 1997, where she won the graduate writing awards for best short story and overall body of fiction. Her short stories have since appeared in several magazines, including the Harvard Review, Salmagundi, Seattle Review, Black Warrior Review, *and* The Hudson Review. *She teaches fiction workshops at the University of the Arts in Philadelphia and the New School in New York City. Currently she is working on her third novel, forthcoming from Simon & Schuster in 2007.*

LUNCH TIME

David Ebershoff

"You want to know about *what*?"

"Sanitation. In the subway system."

"Oh no, we ain't supposed to talk about that." The supervisor is almost sixty, wears blue pants and a blue sports shirt (the sort-of uniform of the subway system's sanitation workers), and oversees a cleaning crew of up to ten, depending on the shift. Her eyes are small, quick, and friendly. Her girlish chuckle betrays what she thinks of the MTA's rules that keep her from talking about its garbage. When I ask her name she wags a finger in the air. "Oh no, I can't tell you that."

"What about your job, what you do? Can you talk about that? How you clean the station?"

"I don't clean the station."

"What do you do?"

"I wipe down the turnstiles."

"What do you use to wipe them down?"

"Nu-Sheen."

"N-E-W—"

"N-U-" another woman interrupts. She's been hanging around, curious about my conversation with her boss. She's also in blue pants and a blue sports shirt, although hers is oversized and hangs to her thighs. She's forty-two years old, on the other side of 200 pounds, and follows the cues from her supervisor about how much she can say about how they clean a subway station.

"N-U-S," the supervisor adds.

"That's right."

"Does it work?" I ask.

The supervisor moves closer to me. "It work all right."

"I wipe 'em down," the second woman says, "and get rid of that stank."

"How often do you clean the turnstiles?"

"No," the supervisor says. "We wipe 'em down then go on to the next station. Nine to five."

"How many stations do you clean in a shift?"

"Three or four."

"That's right," the woman in the baggy shirt says. "Sometimes four." I ask her name but she shakes her head and averts her eyes as if to say, Please don't ask me that.

"Does every station have a space like this for you to work out of?"

We are standing in a wide, clean corridor behind a steel door that says TA EMPLOYEES ONLY and lists two 718 numbers for emergency electrical maintenance. We are directly beneath the shuttle platform, across from the turnstiles, at the Franklin Avenue Station in Crown Heights. The floors are poured concrete and the walls are concrete block painted beige. It looks like a passageway beneath the bleachers at a basketball arena. Another crew member enters the corridor from an interior door. He is fifty-five but looks fifteen years younger. He is strong and fit, with pistonic forearms. Amber-lensed sunglasses sit atop his gleaming, shaved head. He mostly listens to his colleagues and nods when he agrees with them. Sometimes he says, "Yeah." His name is Dwight, except that's not his real name. The woman in the baggy shirt accidentally called him by his real name and then made me promise not to write it down.

"Where do you store your cleaning supplies?"

"Right there." The supervisor points to three yellow buckets with aerosol cans of Nu-Sheen in them. "Here our rags." She points inside a garbage pail on wheels. "See 'em?"

There they are.

"See how dirty they are?"

Indeed.

"What do you have to clean up the most?"

This sets off a rift on litter:

"Bottles, cans, bags—"

"Lots of bags, especially from Duane Reade."

"Cups, caps, and gum."

"Cigarettes."

"*Lots* of cigarette butts."

"Liquor bottles."

"Lots of those."

"And paper."

"Lots of paper."

"Where all that paper come from?"

"Most especially toilet paper."

"Oh and Metrocards."

"All over. Dang Metrocards."

Then I ask: "What's the worst thing you have to clean up?"

The supervisor doesn't hesitate: "Feces. You know what I'm saying?"

Her colleagues are silent: not much else to say about that.

I must be making a prissy face because the supervisor adds, "Every day." She folds her arms and looks me up and down and I would guess she's thinking something along the lines of, *I'd like to see Miss Thing here clean that up.*

"What's the worst station to clean?" I go on.

In chorus: "All of 'em."

"What's the worst borough to clean?"

"All of 'em."

"This is a pretty nice station, isn't it?"

"That's because we just cleaned it," says Dwight.

"Come back in a few minutes," the supervisor advises and then chuckles.

"New Yorkers are messy?"

Her eyebrows shoot up.

"How can New Yorkers help keep the stations clean?"

"Don't litter," she says pragmatically.

"That's right," says the second woman. "They need to clean up behind themselves."

"I be sweeping up," says Dwight, "and someone comes along and drops his trash right where I finished or they throw their trash on the ground when the trash can's right there." He points to the barrel on wheels.

"That's the worst," says the supervisor. Then she shrugs. "This station ain't so bad. They renovated it. Could be better, but it ain't so bad."

"Except it stanks downstairs." The woman in the baggy shirt looks at her boss to see if she's said too much.

"Yeah, what is that?" When I got off the C train I definitely noticed an odor that smelled like, well, butt.

"That's the oil from the elevator," the supervisor says.

"It stanks."

Then it occurs to the supervisor that I might have some influence with the MTA, or politicians, or someone. "Tell 'em we need more workers."

"You need more workers?"

The two women say "Yes" and Duane says "Yeah."

"How many?"

"A lot. We always need more."

Earlier, when I called the MTA's office of Public Affairs, a spokesman told me they wouldn't answer my questions about sanitation. How many employees? Can't say. How much garbage is removed? Can't say. What are the tools of the trade? Silence and a sigh that could be interpreted as: I don't have time for this. I asked if I could follow a sanitation worker around for a while and was told no. Why not? "Because they're doing their *job*." This is one of the aftermaths of 9/11 and the London tube bombings. Any basic information about public infrastructure theoretically could be used by terrorists. This might seem a little silly until you realize that an aerosol can of, say, Nu-Sheen is a perfect device to distribute sarin gas in an enclosed environment.

"When you ride the subway when you're not working, do you notice all the garbage or do you just zone it out?"

"I don't ride the subway," the supervisor says. "It's dirty. When I'm outta here, I'm out. I rather use the bus. The bus is clean, you know what I'm saying? It's clean like Disneyworld. You been to Disneyworld?"

Although I've never been to Disneyworld, I say that I have. I'm not sure why.

"Then you know what I'm talking about. You see how nice it is? Like the bus."

I ask the other woman the same question and she says she too likes the bus. I ask Dwight but he begs off the question by waving his hand near his face. I should say that Dwight is the reason I'm having this conversation. As I was transferring from the C to the Franklin Avenue shuttle (one of the most charming lines in the system) I saw him near the escalator in a safety-orange vest. I asked if he'd be willing to answer a few questions. He pointed to the door with the employees only sign: "Talk to her?" "Back there?" He opened the door and led me to his supervisor. Then he retreated to an interior room, returning only after his boss started talking to me.

"What's the toughest season to do this job?"

"All seasons is hard," the supervisor says.

The second woman says, "I'm so ready to put my coat back on.

All winter long I was ready to take it off but now that it's hot I'm ready to be cold again." It's a hot, soupy day in August and I feel exactly the same way.

"In winter," says the supervisor, "you got to dress right. The homeless taught me how to dress. They said put newspaper in the bottom of your shoes."

"Inside your shoes?"

"That's right. My feet never get cold in winter. The homeless know about that."

It's at this point that I ask them their ages. They laugh, the way almost everyone past a certain age—40?—laughs when asked this question. I tell them they all look a lot younger. I'm sure this sounds like a writer's flattery but it's true.

"It doesn't age you," says the woman in the baggy shirt. "They look young, that's right, but it doesn't age you."

"It's the way you carry yourself," says the supervisor.

How long have they worked for the MTA?

"Too long," the supervisor says.

"Is it a good place to work?"

"It's all right," she admits. "It's all right." She pauses and thinks about something—I wish I could tell you what—and then looks to her colleagues. "You know what? He's taking up my lunch time."

She opens the steel door and returns to the turnstiles. Her colleagues follow, and so do I.

David Ebershoff is the author of two novels, The Danish Girl *and* Pasadena. *He is an editor-at-large at Random House, and is finishing a new novel,* The 19th Wife. *He can be reached at www.ebershoff.com.*

Metro Blues, or How I Came to America

Boris Fishman

In October 2004, on the eve of the centennial of the New York subway, the Czech-born photographer Peter Peter published "The Subway Pictures," a survey of the system. The images are marvelously spare, the camera concerned with little besides the often extraordinary attributes of ordinary subway riders. Peter's approach makes sense: The most noticeable thing about the New York subway is the people who ride it. Otherwise, it's pretty unremarkable down there—nondescript station walls, orderly Metrocard lines, battleship-gray train cars delivering passengers from one place to another.

If you're looking for a less purely utilitarian experience, the subway's aesthetics don't encourage it. There are the imaginatively whimsical, if diminutive, Arts for Transit installations—the "Lariat Seat Loops" around the station columns at 33rd Street; the nearly two hundred silhouettes of New Yorkers "Carrying On" at Prince Street; and the inevitable curlicues of graffiti. For the most part, however, a New York subway ride, for all its heat and overcrowding, is the height of functionalist banality, and the city's inhabitants are largely sanguine about the experience.

Eighteen years ago, on my first trip down below, this was a shock. Just days before, my family had completed a three-month immigration to New York from the Soviet Union. Before departing, in September 1988, on a westbound train from Minsk, my hometown and the capital of what is now independent Belarus, we traveled to Moscow to arrange our immigration papers. Minsk, which had been occupied by the Nazis, was virtually leveled during World War II, giving its postwar satraps a clean slate to reconstruct the city according to the architectural dictates of socialist realism. Stadium-size concrete boxes squatting on concrete pillars in enormous, windswept plazas became its most distinguishing features. Its thoroughfares—eight lanes wide to accommodate Soviet tanks in case of "imperialist aggression" by the Americans—made the homicidal circle around the Arc de Triomphe in Paris seem like a country road.

The train from Minsk arrived at Moscow's appropriately named Belorussky Depot, which has two adjacent namesakes belonging to two different lines that are part of Moscow's subway system (Metro, from the French *métropolitain*, in Russian). In a kind of reversal of Vladimir Nabokov's 1938 short story "A Visit to the Museum," where the eponymous activity physically transports the protagonist, an emigre, to a pre-Soviet Russia, I felt like the train from Minsk to Moscow's Belorusskaya Stations essentially airlifted me from a postapocalyptic Soviet wasteland to a museum. In one of the Belorusskayas (in Russian, "station" is female, whereas "depot" is male), the pylons of the station-hall were finished with rose and black marble; the chessboard-square floor was marble as well. In the other Belorusskaya, which was lit by vase-shaped lanterns made of glass and marble, the ceilings arched toward decorative bas-reliefs, the central one featuring twelve motifs from Belarussian life. The passageway between the two stations housed a monumental sculpture commemorating anti-Nazi resistance in Belarus during

WWII. However, as we shuttled between the immigration agency, an uncle's apartment where we were staying, and sites in the city, the Belorusskayas came to seem like some of central Moscow's humblest stations.

At Ploshchad' Revoliutsii (Revolution Square), dozens of bronze statues anchored the curved portals (made of red, black, and light-gold marble) leading from the center hallway to the train platform. They formed a narrative of Soviet progress, from Civil War soldiers strapped with ammunition belts to engineers with building plans; laborers with hydraulic drills; and farmers working with wheat to scholars poring over books; parents playing with children; and students tracing the contours of the USSR on a globe. The above-ground entrance to Krasnye Vorota (Red Gates), where the ancient gates to the city of Moscow once stood, was a futuristic series of concentric semicircles expanding from the ground with modernist flair; from the side, the structure resembled a giant telescope, rising submarinelike from below. Komsomolskaya (after Komsomol, the Communist Youth League), one of the first stations built, had side balconies dressed in brown-gold marble and soaring columns with Corinthian cornices decorated with hammer-and-sickle designs and red stars.

I was awestruck.

The Moscow metro was the Soviet Union's consciously created self-creation myth. Built in the 1930s, the system presented the recently established leaders of the new Soviet state with the unique opportunity of an institution that could be Soviet from scratch, without any of the ideological compromises required by existing pre-Soviet structures. The project's leaders knew that the metro would be built with Western technology—Moscow's was the fifteenth metro system in the world. (Besides, the three Soviet engineers who had experience with subway tunneling all happened to be in jail for "economic sabotage.") But if the means had to be borrowed from the West, the meaning would be entirely Soviet. The Moscow metro would demonstrate the singularity and supremacy of the Soviet experiment through the one element that London, Berlin, and New York had neglected: its appearance.

The grandiosity of the task seems only more staggering considering the meager means at the state's disposal. Facing a shortage of concrete, administrators demolished four Moscow churches. The construction of the first station, Sokolniki, in November 1931, proceeded with a workforce of twelve (!) men hacking uselessly at the frozen topsoil with pickaxes and shovels, in possession of neither the pumps to clear the waterlogged soil nor even a building plan showing where they would dig next.

By 1934, the metro consumed a fifth of the city's budget, station aesthetics reportedly claiming 75 percent of that amount. Crystal for the chandeliers, bronze, brass, and rare woods—not to mention twenty-three types of marble—were rushed from the Urals, Siberia, the Caucasus, and Belorussia. "The Metro should be built so that it is beautiful," said Lazar Kaganovich, Commissar of Transportation and Director of Metro Construction, who personally managed the twelve architectural studios he established for the project. The commemorative 1936 publication "The Architecture of the Moscow Metro" put it more poetically: "[I]n every piece of marble lies the soul of a new man."

This marble was meant to "move [the new man of Moscow] through the city ideologically as well as physically," as an official assessment had it, and the stations fulfilled this double duty—ideological enlightenment by means of aesthetic grandeur—with spellbinding effect. Mayakovskaya, built in 1938 as part of a second line of stations, featured columns lined in green-pink marble and stainless steel and, even more strikingly, a ceiling panorama of miniature mosaics tiled into thirty-six oval cupolas. In one, jets soared protectively over the Kremlin; in another, Soviet athletes pursued world records; elsewhere a lean, muscular woman directed an enormous tractor through a field of grain, a red kerchief at her neck and the Soviet flag at her back. Mayakovskaya was so sumptuous that in November 1941, when the war had made aboveground gatherings risky, the Soviet leadership celebrated the twenty-fourth anniversary of the Bolshevik Revolution there. "It is the first subway in which beauty has been attempted," marveled Harold Denny, the *New York Times* reporter in Moscow. By 1936, official Soviet literature commonly referred to the stations as "palaces."

In this case, popular devotion did not have to be decreed from above. Though subsequent lines—a second was built in the late 1930s, a third during World War II, and the fourth mostly in the 1950s—favored occasionally kitschy monumental propaganda over the sleek, spare modernism of the first line, Muscovites developed an affection for the metro provoked by few other Soviet institutions. Its opulence and reliability—"It's one of the few things in Russia that works," as a Moscow curator of an exhibit about the metro remarked in 1994—evoked loyalty even when the awesome fraud of the Communist experiment had made irredeemable cynics of virtually the entire Soviet population.

In the early days, there was a sense of personal investment: 75,000 people helped build the metro, with another 100,000 volunteering on weekends without pay. In later years, it became the rare place where the Soviet citizen, otherwise forced to live a double life of faked enthusiasm, could for a moment feel a harmony between his private and public self; where even the Soviet dream remained alive (and, these days, where pensioners made obsolete by the rapacity and amnesia of the post-Soviet order feel less unwanted). In the humiliating, divisive struggle that was aboveground life, Soviet citizens pillaged every imaginable aspect of the state—the state had denied them any sense of ownership and, in any case, gave them few other means of survival—but they treated the metro like a museum.

I doubt I registered much of the metro's ideological symbolism when I visited; at the age of nine, it struck me as a wonderland, a monument to beauty. It was a place where a government had elected to honor the heart and soul on par with politics and profit, though I wouldn't understand the uniqueness of this kind of worldview for years. There was nothing about my homeland that I would miss more after moving to the United States.

I spent my initial tour of the New York subway system somewhat perplexed; where *was* everything? Where were the chandeliers and bas-reliefs, the sepulchral, pious stillness?

The masterminds of the New York subway had also imagined their system as a landmark of civic art, a testament to New York's increasing prominence in world affairs. William Barclay Parsons, the chief engineer, toured European stations with an eye for design; August Belmont, the main private financier, set aside half a million dollars for station decoration. (Notably, Belmont, like the other great booster of the subway, former Mayor Abram S. Hewitt, was an unabashed Brahmin, disdainful of the recent influx of immigrants partly for whose benefit the subway was being built. The subway was meant to disperse the unsanitary slums where immigrants crowded because less dense parts of the city weren't easily reachable.)

C. Grant LaFarge, the architect, decided on classical gravitas; New York's elites were too *nouveau riche* to appreciate the art-nouveau experimentation of the Paris and Vienna systems. Some of the results were quite striking: the City Hall station featured chandeliers, Romanesque vaults of Guastavino tile, and skylights of leaded glass. The Astor Place station received a *kushk*, a cast-iron and glass kiosk modeled on entrances to the Budapest subway. For the station at 72nd Street and Broadway, LaFarge designed a lovely Flemish Renaissance control house. More than a dozen stations featured decorative panels, Norman brick wall bases, faience or terracotta cornices, and wide ornamental moldings and rosettes on the ceilings. At Astor Place, the ceramic mosaic depicted a beaver, an acknowledgment of John Jacob Astor's fortune in furs. At Clark Street in Brooklyn, there was a festive mosaic of a church spire, trees, and two steamships, in a nod to the nearby wharves.

On October 27, 1904, recently elected Mayor George McClellan inaugurated the new system by steering a wagonload of VIPs from City Hall toward Harlem. Some of the mandarins were skeptical. One of the passengers regretfully noted that the ceiling was the color of a battleship: "If there was a Russian Admiral on this train he'd pull out his revolver and pump holes in that ceiling!" the next day's *New York Times* recorded him saying. A visiting Congressman from Chicago was even more critical: "You ride like the wind, but it smells like a cellar."

Most of the stations were so relatively unadorned that the city's eye doctors publicly expressed concern about the glare produced by the blindingly white walls as the trains sped by, but, glancing out of the car, the VIPs were more peeved by something else. Leaning against the station walls for mounting by workmen, who had already drilled holes in LaFarge's delicate tilework, were three-foot commercial advertisements in cheap tin frames. There was the Coke Dandruff Cure, Evans Ale ("Live the Simple Life"), and, should the ale cause problems, Hunyadi Janos, "A Positive Cure for Constipation." McClellan was outraged, but the logic of capitalism would carry the day: the ads, arranged by Belmont, stayed, as they guaranteed a modest return of the subway's bonded debt.

In the first days, riders seemed to resent the eyesore as well, turning the ads toward the wall or tipping them over, but they gave up soon enough. There was, after all, nothing extraordinary about the subway, as the *New York Times* reported with a little surprise already on its first day:

It was astonishing, though, how easily the passengers fell into the habit of regarding the Subway as a regular thing. While the crowds above were still eagerly watching the entrances to see men emerge, were still enthralled by the strangeness of it all, the men on the trains were quietly getting out at their regular stations and going home, having finished what will be to them the daily routine for the rest of their lives. It is hard to surprise New York permanently.

This was a sign of things to come. By 1905, workers were already removing the elegant *kushks*—they obstructed views of traffic and blocked the sidewalk. (The handsome kiosk visible today at Astor Place is actually a re-creation.) The City Hall station closed in 1945, due to inadequate use and structural shortcomings. Future subway expansions—a second stretch of construction from 1907 to 1913 brought the subway to the outer boroughs, and a third from 1932 to 1940 multiplied the routes—featured largely functional station designs without much concern for aesthetics. (Though a ubiquitous ad urged New Yorkers to take the subway to Flushing Meadows for the 1939 World's Fair, it would be the Moscow metro's Mayakovskaya station that would win the Fair's Grand Prix.) By the 1960s, the original LaFarge mosaics from the first line were disappearing, as part of renovations. Even before, they were virtually ignored. When, in 1957, a subway rider called the Transit Authority public relations office to inquire about the mosaics, the TA publicity man was baffled: "What mosaics? In our subway?"

In 1936, a group of left-wing artists sponsored by the Works Progress Administration (WPA) had tried to reverse the trend. "Here, in the largest, richest, most complex and interesting city in the world, the subjects of the decorative plaques are a beaver, a ferry boat and the cupola of City Hall!" the group's chairman exclaimed to the press. Disparaging New York subway aesthetics as unimaginative and unsuited to the task of uplifting the weary rider—the Moscow subway was approvingly cited as a counterexample—the artists produced proposals for socially conscious artworks celebrating subway construction and pillorying the capitalist rat race. City fathers were horrified: "Never have I seen such uncanny, uncouth and unkempt men and women as these pictures portray, in the agony of their horrible huddle under the ground," a deputy mayor remarked. The idea went nowhere.

Graffiti artists besieged the system in the 1970s, both as vandalism by an urban underclass stymied by the growing gap between rich and poor and as a means of artistic expression, and, in 1985, with the Arts for Transit program, the Metropolitan Transit Authority finally realized that station aesthetics were essential to creating the impression of a safe and reliable subway. But, after the subway's first years, there have never really been large-scale, top-down attempts to endow the system with cultural ballast, with meaning beyond its function as transport. (What few attempts there were always came from well outside the mainstream.) America wasn't really the place for that sort of thing.

In 2000, I returned to the former Soviet Union for the first and only time since my family left. In my first years in the United States, I had studiously neglected my heritage; I was working hard to become an American. Eventually, my background became less threatening, and I started rediscovering Russian culture, even majoring in Russian literature in college. A return was inevitable, and I would spend the summer of 2000 working for the American embassy in Moscow.

Once there, I didn't have to wait long for a Proustian frisson: Entering the metro on the way from Sheremetyevo airport, I nearly buckled from the scent of the escalator lubricant. A commentator on the Moscow-metrophiles' Web site *metro.ru* lovingly notes its "melancholy escalators," and, as risible as such comments may seem to foreign riders, I experienced the encounter more deeply than I had been touched in more than a decade of American life. That smell was an ineffable, olfactory distillation of . . . home.

The following weeks were less welcoming. I wasn't as impressionable as I had been in 1988, and Moscow, always known for a capital's self-importance and coarseness, had become furious. The intervening years of political and economic exploitation by corrupt insiders had produced humiliating, divisive inequality; the metro was as stunning as I remembered, but the faces in the cars were haggard, embittered, and quick to aggression. I was maligned as a Jew;

a traitor who had abandoned his country; an imperialist whose embassy residence had been sacrilegiously built on what was once the Czar's hunting grounds. There were plenty of moments like that first step into the subway but, for the most part, Moscow was a place forced to endure sadistic privation by a coterie of princes who reaped the nation's riches and demonized outsiders for their citizens' hardships. Exiting a metro car on the way to work one morning, I—trained by what is more or less a ritual of the New York subway—offered to help a young woman with a baby carriage at the bottom of a long stairway. She stared at me with dull surprise. "Nobody does that anymore," she said.

In a kind of ode to the Moscow metro the Russian novelist Victor Pelevin, who has made a career of ingenious satires on Soviet and post-Soviet life, wrote in the Swiss newspaper *Neue Zurcher Zeitung* in 2001:

> "[The metro's aboveground] station entrances look like tiny mausoleums, but, at the same time, Lenin's mausoleum looks like a metro entrance. Actually, the entire metro, which has long been named after Lenin, is a virtual mausoleum—the mausoleum of an idea, the mausoleum of the future, the mausoleum of a dream" [translation mine].

The Soviet Union is certainly extinct, but I would disagree with Pelevin's broader point. The Soviet idea is far from dead, perhaps because, catastrophically, it's a quintessentially Russian idea that predated the Soviets by many centuries. I saw it in the Moscow metro in 2000 and you can see it just as easily almost anywhere you look in Russia today, whether you see the oligarch Mikhail Khodorkovsky imprisoned after a show trial for daring to challenge the Putin political machine, or Duma parliamentarians urging the ban of Jewish organizations on the grounds of their adherence to a religion "anti-Christian and inhumane, whose practices extend even to ritual murders."

Russia has almost never belonged to the Russian people; instead, historically, its bounty has been hoarded by a select few who exploited the motherland's name to rally the citizenry to the frequently catastrophic causes they conjured. For all its otherworldly beauty, the Moscow metro, which was built on the backs of ordinary men and women—who were requisitioned for the task like serfs but nonetheless believed in its promise with all their hearts—doesn't belong to its people. It belongs to an eternal idea of Russian supremacy that happily swallows its own. The state actually imagines this cult of Saturn-like self-immolation to be essential to that idea's vitality. One can't imagine graffiti artists widely using the Moscow metro as a canvas for socioeconomic frustration or artistic expression, or a municipal agency encouraging contemporary artists to improve station design. The Moscow metro is a museum, and don't you dare touch anything.

No, graffiti art and Arts for Transit, however banal they may have initially seemed to foreigners like me, could only happen in New York. Here, municipal benefactors who openly disdain immigrant interlopers build transit systems partly for their benefit, whereas in Russia the nation's leaders pretend to build in the name of the people while in reality leave them with nothing. The Muscovites may love their subway more than New Yorkers, but they own it less.

There was no frisson when I entered the subway after disembarking at John F. Kennedy Airport from Moscow that 2000 summer, but there was something equally meaningful. The gray car slowly rumbled into view and came to a halt with a sclerotic sigh. It wasn't much to look at. But it was mine.

Boris Fishman *is the editor of* Wild East: Stories from the Last Frontier. *He has written for* The New Yorker, The New York Times Magazine, The New Republic, The Nation, *and other publications.*

Sources:

Brooks, Michael W. *Subway City: Riding the Trains, Reading New York.* New Brunswick, NJ: Rutgers University Press, 1997.

Couture, Andrea M. "Moscow Metro: A Look Back and Forward," *Mass Transit,* May, 1994, p. 22.

Fischler, Stan. *The Subway: A Trip Through Time on New York's Rapid Transit.* Flushing, NY: H & M Productions II Inc., 1997.

Hood, Clifton. *722 Miles: The Building of the Subways and How They Transformed New York.* Baltimore: The Johns Hopkins University Press, 1993.

O'Donnell, Anne K. "The Moscow Metro, or The Experience of Socialist Realism Underground." Unpublished senior thesis, Princeton University, Princeton, NJ, 2002.

AN EGG SALAD SANDWICH ON THE RED LINE

Anastasia M. Ashman

The summer I graduated from college a high school friend from California came to visit me in Manhattan. We had been close out west, but while I had been slaving in the academy at Bryn Mawr the younger girl had been drifting, partying, burning out. Junior college, career false starts, an indifferent musician boyfriend. Once vibrant, now she seemed undirected in life, lost at eighteen. I didn't know what to do with her.

A former partner of mine in popular-girl crime, she had morphed from a cat-eyed, slinky bon vivant into a person ungainly in her own skin, looking almost Hawaiian with her deep tan and flowered shirts. Extra pounds aside, she seemed vulnerable in ways I had never detected when she zipped around San Francisco in her red Alpha Romeo, a privileged, pretty young thing. Out of her element and on foot in Manhattan, my West Coast guest succumbed to blisters caused by impractical sandals and hobbled into a sedentary routine. Holed up in my steamy, cramped sixth-floor walk-up on Houston Street, she would doze in my bed while I was at work, resting up for

153

our nights on the town, answering my telephone and taking incomplete messages.

If it weren't clear enough already, she let me know that her future was in my hands. It would be great if I could get her a job, she said, as if I had strings to pull. As if my hand-to-mouth bohemian lifestyle was a pose, as if I had chosen for color the one-armed Native American drunk next door who bounced against my wall late at night. August weeks passed and my scruffy Greenwich Village tenement grew smaller. So we kept moving, going to party after party even though things had become strained in our moments alone, even though she was a wide-eyed wallflower before the drinks kicked in. She needed to be dissuaded from moving to New York on a depressed whim. I bided my time, hoping that this intense city that had lured her here would repel her somehow.

We headed uptown one sweltering night with a distinct lack of festivity. The subway car was an oven, an older red one with patchy linoleum flooring that sank down when we stepped on board. We took a seat just inside the door. A dozen New Yorkers were sitting in bubbled spaces on long benches that stretched the length of the ancient car, not looking at each other.

But it was hard not to notice the one person standing by the middle doors, holding on to a pole with one hand, and an egg salad sandwich with the other. He must have been four hundred pounds. Shaped like Humpty Dumpty, his bulk was topped with a blue baseball cap, pasty face darkened with new beard growth. With each bite, his brown eyes rolled upward, as if in ecstasy.

Then, without warning, he vomited. An arc of egg salad projected at least three feet into the center of the car. The volume he regurgitated must have totaled ten egg salad sandwiches, yellow slop spreading in a wide diameter on the patchwork surface.

My guest winced and stared while hardened New Yorkers swiftly got up from their seats and exited at both ends of the moving car. No one spoke, and no one looked back.

The man remained motionless at the pole, as if nothing had

happened. When he took another bite of his sandwich, a gurgling noise escaped from the depths of my poor Californian friend. She wasn't prepared to face this kind of emptiness. I grabbed her arm and pulled her into the next car.

The following day while I was at work she made arrangements to fly home. When she left she didn't look back.

A cultural essayist specializing in tales of personal adventure, **Anastasia M. Ashman** *co-edited* Tales from the Expat Harem: Foreign Women in Modern Turkey *(Seal Press 2006). She has appeared in publications worldwide, from the* Asian Wall Street Journal *to the* Village Voice. *Currently living in Istanbul with her Turkish husband, she is at work on a travel memoir,* Berkeley to Byzantium: The Reorientation of a West Coast Adventuress. *When in New York, she's loyal to the N and the R.*

CUPS

Amy Holman

One morning a few years ago I stood on the F train with my half-empty coffee in front of a row of seated passengers. Since I have for many years walked my hyperactive golden retriever while drinking a cup of coffee, I am confident in the comparatively sedate lurching subway. Yes, I do know there is a rule against eating or drinking on the train. Yes, but a cup of coffee on the morning subway was a necessity for a while there, a bitter consort for the unpromising day ahead. A man and a woman got on the train and stood at the pole between the doors. Here was a couple that belonged in a movie, so styled and de-lighted with each other, matched in appearance— dark hair, bright teeth, clear skin, black-and-white attire. She wore a tight printed dress and a white cardi-gan on her curves, and he wore a black suit made of a material that was like a moonless night in a forest. I have never seen a black suit like that, made from a place rather than a fabric, with depth more than shade. It shamed all other black suits, and had not a speck on it—crumb, curl of fur, strand of hair—nada. The lovers held on to that pole and laughed together, impeccable in their dress, rhythmic in their conversation.

It was one of those stations where you change for something else, almost anything else. The man was getting off, and so apparently was the old fellow in the corner seat near me, as he suddenly realized almost too late. The lovers tasted each other before the parting, which ended just as the old guy knocked into me like a swimmer pushing the water out of his way with his arms, although I was standing off to the side not in his way. While he came across graceless and inconsiderate, it was my coffee that traveled in an arc out of the sipping square of the lid onto the immaculate black suit jacket of the handsome man exiting the train. I made a noise like a Basenji, an alert that would have morphed into the English language if he had turned. He did not hear me, striding toward the other track with his perfect black briefcase swinging, nor did he apparently feel anything, such as the drops of light-coffee-no-sugar decorating his shoulder and back. My mouth would not close. Turning to face the man's girlfriend, I saw that her eyes were turned downward in contentment, lovely and amusing thoughts cavorting in her mind. Sex on the brain, lucky her, and so I sat down in the seat recently emptied. I looked around at the others, expecting disapproval, but no one had noticed anything. Then, I saw the man opposite me in the corner seat next to the window with a book open, a strange smile on his face. His eyes did not seem to be looking at the pages of his paperback, but to be averted from elsewhere in the car, and his expression was one of relish. I kept staring at my one connection to the crime, willing him to look up and recognize my shame and shake his head or scowl. But he was far too pleased to let my sorrow get in the way of a slapstick interlude.

When I was in the ninth grade, I saw Dom DeLuise recount an on-set story on either Merv Griffin or Mike Douglas. It was the shower scene in the madcap *Silent Movie*, directed by Mel Brooks, and filled with cameos by major movie stars. Massive Dom and big-eyed

Marty Feldman were supposed to get in the large posh shower with Burt Reynolds and surprise him by being two additional sets of hands lathering him in the steam. They had to be as naked as possible and when Wardrobe gave them their cover, they were shocked. Dom did his best expression of comic insult, and said, "It was a Dixie cup!" When I told my friends this story, Dixie Cup became our code for penis.

There are those times when we are all of us fragile, betrayed, and lingering in old psychic assaults. Maybe we travel to work some mornings from sessions with therapists and are unready for the daily trials, such as talking on the phone to writers with afflictions of the inner clock—no timepieces, and forlorn life stories that precede questions. The train ride is the transition, a series of lurch and slide movements across the seats that help us to get a better grip. So, of course, I was treated on one of these sensitive travels to work to a full display of an excited man on the 4 train speeding downtown. It was not a well-populated car. When I heard the sound of an injured man to my right, across the doors, I turned to look, and his Dixie Cup was a Slurpee. It's just not the time or the place, really, the person, or the issue—and certainly not the issuing from the person. I scoffed and turned away, yet did not move. But my disdain was nonetheless too much for the man to bear. He got off at the next stop, by which I mean, of course, he left.

On the 6 train, speeding downtown a dozen years ago, my friend Susie and I were sitting across from a mother and her two young sons. It was winter and the light in the train was yellow like urine, and I have a picture to prove it. Susie was at the time a photo editor for *The Providence Journal,* and had her Nikon with her at all times. I had my Canon, and there are pictures of each of us, so much younger than we are now, sitting on the orange and yellow seats in the tinkle-yellow glow of the subway car. The older of the two boys had to go badly, periodically expressing this quietly to his mother in a whisper and furrow of brow, arch of back, cup of the hand over crotch we all of us recognize the world over. She would comfort him but make him wait, softly suggesting home. At her feet were a number of white plastic grocery bags. Her littler boy sat staring off into space, stunned oblivious with exhaustion, while the six- or seven-year-old did his best to calm down. Finally his mother must have realized that one too many arches and cups of the hand signaled imminent spill, and realized she had with her the solution to the problem. She reached into one of the bags and took out a tall soda cup with lid and straw, took off the lid, dumped the remaining slivers of ice into the bag and set the straw and lid on the seat next to her. The car was not well populated, but Susie and I were sitting directly across with 35mm cameras.

Susie had been to India in our senior year at college when there was the assassination and rioting; she'd photographed Mother Teresa for the paper, and she had told me that you just can't think too much about whether anyone wants you to take a picture of them. You can't be shy. The mother lowered the cup and her son unzipped, standing in front of her. The way her arm was with the hand that held the cup, anyone sitting in the next embankment of seats to her left would have had trouble seeing flesh. He finished, zipped up and slid back into place beside her as relieved as could be, and she put the lid back on the cup and held it on her lap the rest of the ride. You'll have to take my word for this because there isn't a single photograph.

Our subway system is filled with beautiful mosaics, old and recently commissioned—those sea turtles swimming freely out of a spooky submerged tunnel at the Houston Street 1 station, that enormous trout and small square of cherries at Delancey on the F. These artistic image fragments soothe us away from the fact of dirty underground bathroom tile, Norway rats like Tonka trucks, and homeless men and women rattling their paper change cups while pitching their yarns of despair. Leave it to MoMA to seize the beggar's cup for Pop Art. A few years ago, they converted—irony intact—the blue and white "It's a Pleasure to Serve You" coffee cup into a squashed leather version with a zipper. I bought one for a friend leaving the city for a year in case she missed the milieu.

I went to Paris in 2002 to give a poetry reading at a bookstore and I didn't know French, but I did know the basics of underground travel. Before I realized that everywhere I wanted to go was nearby, I took the Métro—no small feat for someone outside of the language—which identifies its train lines by the first and last station name. I have to say I like the Métro, and how you can change for regular trains without spending more Euros. They use space on the cars more efficiently than we do, more room for passengers to sit, no room for teenage acrobats to breakdance and perform back flips in the aisles for a cup of change. In the stations they have vending machines; this is all I ask of the MTA: give me a machine that dispenses three-packs of Madeleines.

On a Sunday not that long ago, I am waiting for the F at Bergen, the tunnel so silent it suggests abandonment. I pace between blue girders and look at the wall of movie posters disguised with graffiti before I notice a paper coffee cup with a red heart perched on the edge of the black cylindrical trash can. Grinning, I turn and look across the tracks to the other platform, then around behind me, but I am alone. Surely there is a camera recording reactions to this installation? I sure wish I had my camera because instead of the usual chubby black NY slogan on the cup, the big red heart is for Jodie Foster. I approach to look closely, but do not touch.

This is one of my childhood reference points popped into the present. I am six months younger than Jodie Foster, six months older than Tatum O'Neal, the two cool girls I wanted to befriend because they were smarter than the adults and acted in movies that weren't really for children. I wasn't allowed to watch most of Jodie's movies (*The Little Girl Who Lived Down the Lane, Taxi Driver, Little Foxes*) and Tatum only made a few, but I followed the news of them, imagined myself as savvy, impenetrable, and adorable as they.

I wanted to be an actress because of them. I saw Jodie once at the old Whole Foods on Prince Street, her hair dyed pale orange, a pair of narrow-framed glasses on her nose. She's the height of a twelve-year-old, and unmistakably Jodie Foster.

When a young woman comes to wait for the F(orever) train, I catch her eye. "Look at that," I say, breaking the rule about speaking to strangers in casual tones, and she turns to look, smirks, and returns to her own thoughts. She's far less impressed than I with this specially manufactured piece of pop culture—or retro pop since Jodie sold her production company and is living her own private life at last, with sons that come from Dixie Cups. When Forever comes, I leave I ♥ Jodie Foster behind because it must exist at a station stop, a pause in time travel, even though I know someone else is going to take it or knock it into the can without noticing. But my message has been delivered, and it is not about being on the precipice of obscurity, or descending into trashy movies, no, it is about living the life I want, never mind how long it took to arrive.

Amy Holman is the author of An Insider's Guide to Creative Writing Programs, *published with Prentice Hall Press in 2006, and the poetry collection,* Wait For Me, I'm Gone, *published with Dream Horse Press. She teaches writers how to get published at The New School University, Spalding University, Hudson Valley Writers Center, Bread Loaf Writers Conference, and others. She is a poet and prose writer living near the F Line in Brooklyn, New York, and her writing been nominated for Pushcart prizes and published in* The Best American Poetry 1999, The History of Panty Hose in America, AWP JobLetter, Poets & Writers *magazine, and many print and online literary journals.*

Is This the Good Samaritan Story?

April Reynolds

Odd what we witness on the subways. Especially considering that ever-popular (yet unsubstantiated by my reckoning) myth: New Yorkers don't notice a thing. Bull. Not my most poetic response, but it is apt. I've caught and dropped the gazes of fellow passengers too often to count. My average thirty-minute commute to work teems with nonverbal communication. To wit: I catch the eye of an African woman with a pale blue plastic bag perched atop her head, her three- and five-year-olds clutching each hand; one is quietly pleading to go to the bathroom. "Pee, pee," he mouths, grimacing, and together we glare at a young woman who has the audacity to bring on a three-carriage stroller burdened with two Citarella grocery bags and a Rite Aid sack full of God-knows-what, but certainly no children. She's taking up three seats. Despite the heavy sighs erupting all around her (we've morphed into the humming section of the Harlem Boys choir), she doesn't look up from her copy of the *Daily News* and refuses to fold away the baby carriage and offer the poor woman or her children (particularly the one swaying back and forth with a full bladder) the empty seats on either side of her.

See, a New York subway moment. And no one said a word.

My years living in this city are replete with such experiences. I would hazard a guess every New Yorker has his or her own private stock of cocktail party–worthy subway stories that fall into three major groups: The stinky story, the Good Samaritan story, and the scary story. These are broad categories that can conflate or morph at will. What begins as a stinky story at Union Square 14th Street on the 4/5/6 can transform into a Good Samaritan story by the 86th Street stop. A ponderous heap on the south end of the car oozing a stench that makes me pray nothing living could be found in its depths while the blackened, calloused foot and slow rustle tells me otherwise, awakening suddenly as the trains hurtles uptown. The lights flicker off for a moment and my fellow commuters and I take the opportunity to move as far away as we can. A number flee to the adjacent car, the rest of us huddle at the far end of the train (I happen to be squeezed next to a guy who either has forgotten to wear deodorant today or simply doesn't bother with such hygienic acts). Only two girls who look to be fifteen or sixteen refuse to move. Well-dressed, manicured, frosted, their clutter of bags reveals their privilege: ZARA, H & M, PINK—stores I don't even bother to window shop. One girl dressed in a lavender silk top leans into her friend and shares what I assume is a joke, since both immediately chortle. They're yapping too loudly to realize the homeless man has woken up and begun gathering his things. We've hit 42nd—commuters quickly peer inside, smell the stench, and go to the next car. He stands, loses his balance, gains it, searches his coat pocket, and takes out what I think is a pee bottle. And then he does the expected: Lurching forward, he calls out in a surprisingly clear voice, "Can somebody help a brother out? I just need some food, man. Can somebody help a brother?" The train seems to mosey from 59th to 86th. "Say, can you help a brother?" He's within reaching distance from the girls. One reaches inside a bag, taking out a cellophane-wrapped sandwich and hands it over. The train pulls into the station. "See ya," they tell him as if they know him. We left in the car are an uncharitable lot, and when the two girls leave, I look around, my thoughts perfectly mirrored on the faces of most passengers: "Tourists."

What began as a stinky story morphed into a Good Samaritan story, though it's not one I tell often. It's obvious I'm not the hero. Worse, I (along with the rest of the passengers, I might add) had committed a cardinal sin: the full-on unmitigated stare. No sidelong glances or quick turns of the head only to immediately drop your gaze into an airplane novel; a couple of us (not me) even had the gall to have our mouths open.

What transpired wasn't that exceptional. A homeless man asked for help and received as much. Something dawned on me when I contemplated the girls' response and ours: They were unafraid. When I think on all of my subway stories, whether smelly or kind or funny, fear plays a pivotal role—take this one for instance: A young Chinese man gets on the train at 103rd Street on the West Side, stands next to me, and plucks a yellow onion from his coat pocket, and proceeds to peel away its outer skin. It's finished in eight bites, and directly afterward something begins to bug him in his pants; he vigorously scratches his crotch, his entire hand disappears. And then, of course, the topper—an unmistakable look of confusion blossoms on his face as the six hands previously holding the pole release it and reach for the ceiling. Stinky and funny. But I had forgotten until now the knot in my throat when I was unsure of what he would pull out of his pocket. My subway experiences hold one common element: fear. It's 2006, but most commuters (me included) still behave as if we inhabit New York circa 1982. Keep your head down and your mouth shut, and pray that when the danger occurs on the subway that it takes place on the other end of the car. A group of teenagers bringing recess voices and playground antics onto the northbound N looks like a roving gang; it's my fear that at any moment a knife will be produced. And I don't think I'm alone. Why is it that the New York commuter psyches can't shake their perpetual skittishness? Our city and subways lost their teeth. Why, even at my most observant, hadn't I noticed?

The subways have become a version of Disneyland, tame yet entertaining. I think on my daily rides to work and compare them to the harrowing tales of the subway in Saul Bellow's *Mr. Sammler's Planet*. Ride the bus in lieu of the train? A man mugging another in broad daylight without a soul coming to help? For Mr. Sammler the imagined trumps the known; what could be found in the bowels of the subway is worse than the real bejeweled pickpocket on the bus. And those cocktail stories we all drunkenly tell, their delivery effusive with laughter, have infected our commuter psyche; as a result a hidden cocked gun lurks in every coat. No wonder I've neglected to see the subway's transformation into a communal journey teeming with muted kindness. I'm still living in my husband's aunt's chilling tales of riding the subway during the '80s, her commute a straightjacket of rules that if broken meant being held up at knifepoint. I compare the past's subway murals of graffiti with what recently occurred—a group of artists asked for a permit to hold a graffiti fair and when denied, instead of spelling out their grievances over the new steel trains, took the mayor to court . . . and won. This is not to say I long for those violent days, but it does make me wonder. When will the average New Yorker behave the way the out-of-towners do: without fear?

April Reynolds has taught at New York University and is currently teaching creative writing at Sarah Lawrence College. Her short stories have appeared in several anthologies. Published by Metropolitan Books/Henry Holt in 2003, her first novel, Knee-Deep in Wonder won the Zora Neale Hurston/Richard Wright Foundation Award and the PEN American Center: Beyond Margins Award. Her second book is forthcoming from Free Press/Simon & Schuster.

SERVICE ADVISORY

Garrett Chaffin-Quiray

My story begins a few years ago upon receiving a commission to write about Michael Winner's 1974 movie, *Death Wish*. Not having seen the movie in years, and unable to recall much about it other than it being the feature debut of Jeff Goldblum, I determined to rent and re-screen the title before putting pen to paper. Unable to find *Death Wish* in my Queens neighborhood, though, I rode the F train to Manhattan's West 4th Street station to visit nearby Kim's Video. Picture this: a white, thirtysomething, glasses-wearing transplant New Yorker rid-ing the subway to rent a movie about a white, forty-something, mustachioed Manhattanite

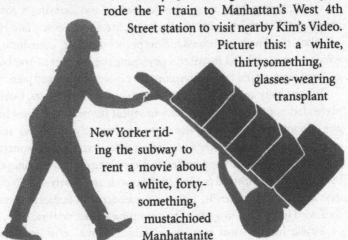

subway vigilante. Faces loom large. Unknown languages herald some foreign-born consortium of assassins hell-bent on doing me harm. Rumble, blur.

The pulse quickened and I arrived at West 4th Street station, released from underground captivity to rent my movie.

To my surprise, *Death Wish* was much better than I remembered it, and this after a long confusion concerning Charles Bronson's believably sympathetic Paul Kersey with later incarnations of the same character in one of the sequels that eventually became both the apex and nadir of his tough-guy movie career. Thus primed to write an essay, I realized I was agitated by some memory released through paroxysms of Mr. Bronson's iconic gunfire.

The mind turns. Memories invade the present and a single incident crystallizes of the moment when I first became aware of the urban jungle as being both wooded and frightening. So it was on the afternoon of December 22, 1984, when Bernhard "Bernie" Goetz boarded the number 2 Seventh Avenue IRT. Already en route that day from the Bronx to Manhattan, where they planned to rob video game machines, were four young black men, Barry Allen, Darrell Cabey, Troy Canty, and James Ramseur.

Goetz, having been mugged twice before, was carrying a concealed pistol, in violation of New York City, State, and Federal law. He was also armed with soft-nosed hollow point bullets, or "dum dums," which were prohibited by treaties governing the conduct of war because of their central purpose: maximum physical injury and pain.

When Canty approached Goetz and asked for five dollars, Goetz pretended not to hear, asked Canty to repeat himself, then drew his gun. Shooting Canty, who was now permanently paralyzed and brain-damaged, Goetz turned on Canty's three companions, wounding each in turn. Afterward he fled to New Hampshire, intending to bury his gun, but instead got lost in the woods and nearly died. Nine days later, on December 31, 1984, he surrendered to authorities and confessed to the shootings, thereby becoming a cause célèbre.

Public reaction was predictably mixed. Some considered the

mild-mannered straphanger a hero. Others thought him an ordinary racist who overreacted to casual elbow rubbing precisely because mild-mannered white people are often closeted racist killers. Divergent opinion notwithstanding, the criminal court's jury acquitted Goetz of most charges, save for illegal weapons possession, sentencing him to eight months in prison. Soon afterward he faced a civil suit filed on behalf of Darrell Cabey, which was resolved after twelve years with a judgment against Goetz, who had since become a vegetarian, an independent political candidate, and an all-around, first-class weirdo.

Be that as it may, in December 1984 I lived in Southern California where Bernie Goetz barely registered among newspaper headlines concerned with drought and illegal migrants. I was eleven years old and in the sixth grade, but Goetz still managed to lodge in my memory for symbolizing New York City through one swift act of defensive violence.

This Goetzian impression ran deep and amplified the previous year's Dirty Harry vehicle *Sudden Impact* (Clint Eastwood, 1983), a family favorite because of "Go ahead, make my day" and because of a country-and-western hit of the same name that had remarkable traction on the radio in our diesel Toyota Corolla. Gradually, though, as Eastwood's Harry turned into Preacher in *Pale Rider* (Eastwood, 1985), thereby unmooring my earlier interest, and as the Goetzian outrage dissolved into adolescence, I developed as finely honed a fascination with New York City as any non-native. Enter my City-itis, best expressed through movies like *The Taking of Pelham One Two Three* (Joseph Sargent, 1974), *King of New York* (Abel Ferrara, 1990), *Just Another Girl on the I.R.T.* (Leslie Harris, 1992), *Money Train* (Joseph Ruben, 1995), *Mimic* (Guillermo del Toro, 1997), and vivid sequences in *Blade* (Stephen Norrington, 1998) and *Spider-Man 2* (Sam Raimi, 2004). In each of these films, the subway is exciting and representative of the American melting pot boiling over, but with *Death Wish* the subway was, first and foremost, a filth-ridden tomb.

Released on July 24, 1974, *Death Wish* exists mostly as a vengeance fantasia writ large over the worst-case scenario of urban professional white male angst. When liberal Manhattan architect Paul Kersey (Charles Bronson) learns that his wife and daughter have been raped, resulting in death and coma, respectively, he turns to the police for help. Unsatisfied with the resulting effort to apprehend his home's invaders, he takes up target shooting while recuperating in Arizona and returns home ready for trouble. Bloodshed ensues, often with particular brio after street thugs mistake Kersey for a patsy. Yet as the dramatic arc transforms virulent social ills into graphically dispatched individual criminals, the subway itself provides the setting for several of Kersey's misadventures before end credits and four sequels turn him into a joke.

As how-to manuals go, Bernie Goetz couldn't have asked for a better primer in urban terrorism, however justified, than Charles Bronson's steely-eyed antihero. That both vigilantes are connected, if only as peculiar correlations in memory—the one imagined, the other real—attacks the old conundrum, does art imitate life, or the reverse?

White and bespectacled as I am, and having been mugged once and verbally harassed on many occasions, I recognize Goetz and his rage when I look in the mirror. I don't know if art imitates life or if life conjures art from authentic experience or if we're lost in a hall of mirrors, endlessly reflecting memories we share as a communal unconscious. But I do know that every story has a beginning, middle, and end, just like movies or when riding a subway.

For me this recognition stems from obsessive theatergoing in film school. Through Mafiosi flicks like *The Godfather* (Francis Ford Coppola, 1972), cop movies like *Serpico* (Sidney Lumet, 1973), science fiction hyperbole like *Escape from New York* (John Carpenter, 1980), and agitprop like *Do the Right Thing* (Spike Lee, 1989), the Big Apple became a concrete and asphalt playground of high-energy heroes and dastardly villains, even as I learned the buzzwords of the academy, like "discourse," "postmodernity," and "identity." Along the way I also amassed useful facts about New York City.

For instance, New York City was almost the U.S. capital, but for colonial-era tensions between northern industrialists who favored the mouth of the Hudson River and southern farmers who preferred Virginia's riverfront for what would become Washington, D.C. Then there is the East River, not really a river at all but a tidal estuary. Or Central Park, neither central nor a park, in the sense of being the city's physical center and natural green space, since the actual center is in Queens and Frederick Law Olmstead so exactly designed Central Park's nature that no tree, rock, walkway, or fallen leaf escaped his designer's eye. Most important of all, I learned about the arterial subway network, with its capillary platforms, stairwells, and tunnels, which offers a biological metaphor that overlaps with cinema.

Certain scholars insist movie theaters are a womb. Dark, temperature-controlled, lined with plush seating, and invisibly wired for sound, they reveal an aperture into an escapist dream and a reflection of our preferred reality. For who claims no satisfaction whatsoever while sitting in bucket seats, holding oversize snacks and feeling one's butt vibrate to the thrum of speakers hidden behind a glittering screen? Inside four walls, encased in concrete and suspending normal rules of order, we become vulnerable and enter a non-space within each auditorium, where we marvel at onscreen adventures in exchange for total confinement.

In this way, the movie-womb non-space is like a casino, hospital waiting room, or a car on a freeway in gridlock. It brings the world to us, does our traveling, busy work, and cleanup, so as to pick the fruits of someone else's labors. Centripetally speaking, it therefore presents us with a piece of the world if we stand still, because the movie-womb is a buffer, packaging experience rather neatly, very much like an aphorism inside a fortune cookie.

But there is a second kind of non-space, offering spectacle and duration, usually without the annoyance of connection to other people. Airline flights and ocean cruises epitomize the model—but then there is the New York City subway.

My favorite is the aforementioned F train from West 4th Street that runs north through Manhattan, east under the East River and into Queens, ending at Forest Hills 71st Avenue. For a while I was partial to the Northbound 6 train from Bleecker Street to 51st Street in Manhattan and there are reasonable arguments for the 1 or 9 train from 116th Street south to 59th Street Columbus Circle and for the majestic three borough passage of the A train from Inwood-207th Street in upper Manhattan, south through Jay Street Borough Hall in Brooklyn, with an eastward bend toward a split terminus in either Far Rockaway Mott Avenue or Rockaway Park Beach 116th Street in Queens.

As of 2005, trips cost $2, meaning there is unlimited use of cars and platforms, as long as one pays admission and doesn't commit a crime. Testing the connective limits of this system has been a worthwhile game for soldiers and sailors on leave since World War I. It's also been a necessary hostel for homeless people in harsh weather.

Subways form the skeleton of New York City, stitching commerce and flow together with people and purpose. It's an experience accessible to all, simultaneously everywhere and nowhere, a conveyance from one named place to another, yet not as a presence in its own right, despite being open 24/7. But subways are also a non-space, neither yours nor mine, where we sit or stand by ourselves, often reading or sleeping, as we travel through a city we sample by looking out at the platform.

At the 81st Street/Museum of Natural History platform on Manhattan's West Side, there is a marine mosaic of tile and concrete directly below the Natural History Museum. At 74th Street/Broadway in Jackson Heights, Queens, Little India sends colorful saris and fragrant naan smeared with lamb curry onto the train. Exiting 161st Street/Yankee Stadium in the Bronx, the platform rises above the predominantly working-class black and Latin neighborhood as frame for the house that Ruth built. Along the rails at Avenue U in Gravesend, Brooklyn, Maurice Sendak's universe falls into smart relief among black-garbed Hasidim living in the row houses radiating away from Coney Island's garish Cyclone. Then there's 34th Street/Penn Station, in Manhattan, with indoor stairwells leading up to Madison Square Garden.

All this recognition spun outward from one writing assignment, but because I'd rented *Death Wish* for only a day, I quickly retraced the morning's journey to avoid a hated late fee. One difference between the two trips: where I was earlier self-consciously aware of potential threats and likewise amused by my oversensitivity, the second trip is pure malevolence, my having been jarred by *Death Wish* and the reinforcement of sifting through memories that reveal Bernie Goetz after twenty years' dormancy. Now the subway is a hassle and irritant, inasmuch as it makes me depend on a conveyance quite totally out of my control.

I count the number of young black men in my subway car and quickly perish the thought; so embarrassing is it to my present person. Then Kersey's big scene in a subway car comes to mind, the one in which he fingers his gun in a coat pocket while carrying a grocery bag—lure for hoodlums drawn to his seemingly defenseless person. Harassed, he doesn't back down and from the screen within my movie memory I again recount the number of young black men on my subway car, now recalling that Goetz dispatched four assailants, almost in a photorealist adaptation of Kersey's subway attack.

But now I'm the paranoid straphanger, consumed by thoughts of another paranoid straphanger while returning a feature film rental about still another paranoid straphanger. Authentic experience reduces to fantasy. Fantasy becomes authentic experience and somewhere in this churn, I return *Death Wish* to Kim's, fully aware that the movie-womb and subway non-spaces have gone supernova, spilling into one another and disturbing an otherwise straightforward writing assignment.

So goes one subway story, a service advisory.

Garrett Chaffin-Quiray was educated at the University of Southern California School of Cinema-Television and has sponsored film festivals, taught writing and media history, and published work in various newspapers, magazines, books, and online journals. He now writes from San Diego County.

IF I WERE IN CHARGE OF THE MTA

Lucinda Rosenfeld

In my everyday life I am mildly libertarian. When it comes to the subway, however, I am one of those people who believes in the rule of law. In this case, the law means New York City Transit's "Rules of Conduct," Section 1050.1 to 1050.12, which forbids everything from riding on the roof to taking up more than one seat. Also on the no-no list are: sleeping, smoking, gambling, panhandling, spitting, urinating, hurling projectiles, carrying box-cutters and open flames, making too much noise, engaging in commercial activities, and skateboarding and/or rollerblading down the aisle.

Some of the fine print can seem excessive—Draconian, even. But then in many respects the subway constitutes its own society, distinct from the one overhead. It contains the same cross-section of races and ethnicities, yet is compressed within borders so narrow that it sometimes seems a small miracle that every rush-hour ride doesn't result in physical violence. After all, in no other aspect of urban life do we find ourselves brushing buttocks with complete strangers reeking of mayonnaise and body odor, and, more than likely, exhausted and cranky from either lack of sleep or from a long day on the job.

I moved to New York City in 1991, and to Brooklyn in 1993. I have been taking the subway to and from Manhattan ever since. I have also spent countless hours on the A train from Brooklyn to the George Washington Bridge Bus Terminal, at 175th Street, en route to my parents' house in New Jersey. Of course, the subway I know today is not the one experienced—and feared—by riders in the 1970s. Today MTA riders benefit from relatively clean cars, and muggings are the exception rather than the rule. Even so, in my fourteen years as a regular MTA customer, there is no aberrant subway behavior I haven't witnessed except, luckily, for assault and murder.

The schoolmarm in me rebels at every breach, from the vaguely annoying to the blatantly disgusting.

The low point was perhaps the snowy February afternoon, several years ago, that I found myself sitting across from a disturbed man who was masturbating inside his snowsuit. Then there was the time that, as I exited an early morning 4 train, a guy who either was or wasn't a pimp asked me, "Baby, how much?" (It took me weeks to recover from that one. On the plus side, I started removing my eyeliner before I went to bed.) Still, neither offense compares to the one experienced by an old roommate, many years ago, in a crowded 1 train on her way to the office. Seated next to her in the car was a man who was bent double over his lap, his head practically hitting the floor. Concerned that he was ill, my friend turned to inspect him—only to find that he had a pocket mirror angled up her skirt.

The panhandlers who call the subway their place of work are upsetting in an entirely different manner. The bourgeois escapist in me wishes they would be gone, sad tales and all, so I can get back to my newspaper (where tales of the poor and unlucky can be mused upon at a palatable remove from reality). When a terrible odor is involved, the feeling is only magnified. In extreme cases, i.e. when fecal matter plays a role, my self-preservationist instinct dictates only that I locate fresh air. Yet, offensive smells aside, the bleeding heart in me aches for their plight and fishes for loose change. This is especially true when there is a physical malady involved. (For years, a man with only a torso "worked" the 2 train, propelling himself on a skateboard.) Inevitably, the two sides end up at war, leading to feelings of agitation. I'm ashamed to report, however, that the escapist side usually wins, bolstered by the admittedly self-serving arguments that (a) the societal failures that have led to this person's unhappy situation will not be rectified by my fifty cents, and (b) the MTA forbids such activities, and the law must be obeyed or chaos will reign.

There are even rules that I wish the MTA *would* adopt, but have so far failed to address. Alcohol is already forbidden, as is the consumption of open beverages. (Who among us MTA riders have not despaired at sitting down in a pool of semi-ossified grape drink!) But, to date, there has been no initiative to address the in-transit consumption of stinky food, such as tuna fish salad sandwiches, Mu Shu pork, and even cheeseburgers and fries. (Yes, there are people who loathe the smell of ketchup.)

Were I in charge of the MTA, I would also likely advocate a No Preachers rule. The problem, for me, is not so much the subject of their sermons as the length of time they go on, and on, and on. Indeed, no one loves the sound of his own voice as much as a Subway Jesus. You might think that it would be in the interest of the preacher to "spread the love" to as many cars as possible. In fact, the sermons typically last all the way back to Brooklyn, and prevent you from having any independent thoughts except, "I wish someone would hit that guy over the head with a baseball bat." This is why, at the first glimpse of a Man of God, I now try to switch cars. Speaking of grating noises, there is also the problem of riders munching on celery and apples—a pet peeve of my brother-in-law.

Finally, I would advocate a "no squeezing into a seat smaller than you are" rule. It's just not fair to the person sitting next to you. It's one thing to brush hips. It's another thing to be sitting in a complete stranger's lap. In a similar vein, the public display of affection, beyond quick smacks and friendly cuddling, should be grounds for a stiff fine and a mandatory hotel room. As for subway "pickups," I admit to having mixed feelings. I know of several happy couples who have met this way. Many years ago, however, I was followed out of the West 4th Street station by a cute medical malpractice lawyer with whom I'd exchanged meaningless eye contact. We actually went on a date. He turned out to be insane.

At my most curmudgeonly, I also wonder if a No Speaking rule wouldn't benefit the city. It's probably unrealistic. But just think how much reading you'd get done.

Lucinda Rosenfeld is the author of the novels What She Saw . . . *and* Why She Went Home. *Her fiction and essays have appeared in the* New Yorker, *the* Sunday Telegraph, New York Magazine, *and* Glamour.

PARNASSUS UNDERGROUND

Patrick Flynn

Every morning at six, I board the Bx34 bus at its terminus in the North Bronx and ride it to Bainbridge Avenue and 205th Street, where I catch the D train. I ride the D down to 145th Street in Manhattan, then change trains and levels for the A uptown to 168th. I am on the subway for fifty minutes. Whenever I describe the trip to someone, the response is always, "I don't know how you do it."

I do it the way a lot of people do it. I read.

I have always done my best reading on the subway. Perhaps the roar of the train acts as a kind of white noise, focusing my attention. For 100 minutes a day, I am in subterranean limbo, freed temporarily from all responsibility. Neither here nor there, I read in peace.

I picked up the habit of subway reading in high school. I worked in an ice-cream shop in Greenwich Village. It was a loose place, staffed by graduate students. Everyone who worked there was teed off about something. Books were the cudgels of long, ringing arguments among the workers. Titles unfamiliar to me were thrown off like beads of sweat. We were paid in cash at the end of each shift, and I would stop at Eighth Street Books in search of some of the titles that had whizzed by me. Some, of course, whizzed too quickly. It turned out not to be *The Coming of Plague to Samoa* and to this day I confuse *Middlemarch* and *Middletown*.

I sat on the IRT on the way home to Flatbush Avenue and read Herbert Marcuse and Thomas DeQuincey, *The Feminine Mystique* and "The Rape of the Lock," James Baldwin and John Barth. I tried to read *Gravity's Rainbow*, which had just come out, but it was too difficult. I read *The Golden Notebook* because it was the favorite novel of the ice-cream store's night manager, with whom I was smitten. She turned out to be gay, and the book troubling: Anna and Molly spoke in the same oblique fashion as the women on the subway whose conversations I happened to overhear. There was much about women that I didn't understand, and Doris Lessing wasn't much help. I read Rimbaud, who was an eye-opener: "Their skulls caked with vague roughness/Like the leprous flowerings of old walls," he wrote in "The Men Who Sit," which could have been titled "The Men Who Sleep on the Seats in the Subway Car."

I was really getting ahead of myself. I hadn't read *Animal Farm*, but I'd read *Down and Out in Paris and London*. *The Jungle* was a mystery to me, but not *The Metropolis*. My reading was skewed. My understanding of the great edifice of literature was weak, though I was familiar with a few gargoyles here and there.

I left New York City for college, but returned in the summer to work as a special officer at Yankee Stadium, which involved breaking up fistfights and ejecting drunks. The Yankees were the big team in town. The crowds at the ballpark were big and salaries were big—it was the era of Steinbrenner and Jackson and Martin, big personalities. My commute was big, too—an hour and three-quarters each way. Big American books only seemed appropriate. I read *Moby-Dick* and *All the King's Men*. I tried to read *Gravity's Rainbow* again, but it was still too difficult.

Not everything I read in that period was American. "The air felt like a warm bath into which hotter water is trickling constantly," wrote E. M. Forster in *A Passage to India*, and there was no better description of life on the 4 train, which still was not air-conditioned. The graffiti had also gotten out of hand. Most outraging was that these artists were turning up in the downtown galleries. John Ruskin, writing of Whistler in "Fors Clavigera," foresaw it all: "I have seen, and heard, much of Cockney impudence before now, but never expected to hear a coxcomb ask two hundred guineas for flinging a pot of paint in the public's face."

Physically, the subway was deteriorating. Breakdowns were constant. I was regularly put off the train in places I would never have dared to go. The stations were gloomy and dangerous-seeming. I was nervous, but I wasn't alone. Waiting with me on those desolate platforms were the people who lived in those terrible neighborhoods, and they were just as frightened as I was. Crime preys mostly on its closest neighbors—a basic lesson, I suppose, but it took signal overhaul and malfunctioning doors for me to grasp it. I read *The Wretched of the Earth* and *The Hidden Injuries of Class*. Someone had scribbled on a poster in the Utica Avenue station: THE POOR YOU WILL ALWAYS HAVE WITH YOU. CAN WE GO TO A MOVIE?

After college, I lived in Borough Park. I worked at various jobs and tried to write. I rode the F train into the city. Most of the other passengers were either Hispanic or Orthodox Jews. It was part of my grand writing plan to minimize distractions by living among people whose cultures were not my own—exile on a shoestring— in Brooklyn. I read *A Moveable Feast* and then everything I could about that Paris crowd. I scoffed at their idea of exile. One American in Paris—that's exile. Thirty Americans in Paris, hanging out at the same cafés and bookshops—that's a package tour. I carped, but secretly I envied. Imagine sitting on the Paris Métro, reading the first edition of *The Sun Also Rises* or *Ulysses*.

I read literary biographies. I felt a kinship with F. Scott Fitzgerald, who'd also had trouble getting a handle on the interplay of life and art. He and I were paralyzed by the same questions: Am I living now? Or just preparing to write? Should I be enjoying this or memorizing it? There was, unfortunately, no biography of Thomas Pynchon, so I gave *Gravity's Rainbow* another shot, with the expected results.

Then I moved to Washington Heights. Now it took me just twenty minutes to get to work. I nearly went berserk. I had no time to read anything. I tried short stories: Saki, de Maupassant, John Cheever. The last depressed me because I thought of long journeys on commuter trains. Cheever's suburban executives had their problems, but if they wanted to, they could read *War and Peace* on their way home.

I have found certain books to be complemented by particular subway lines. Any work concerned with class struggle, from *Das Kapital* to *The Bonfire of the Vanities* could be enjoyed on the Lexington Avenue or Seventh Avenue IRT, since the Upper East and Upper West Sides are merely a stop or two from the South Bronx and passengers are an intriguing mix of the haves and have-nots. *Ragtime*, *A Tree Grows in Brooklyn*, and other evocations of old New York are best savored on the BMT M, which executes a lazy arc over the Williamsburg Bridge and crosses Brooklyn on an elevated structure that passes, in places, not more than five feet from the tenement windows. It seems possible to reach out and lower a window shade. The gulls race the trains and wheel away as the A crosses Jamaica Bay on its way to the Rockaways; one might look up from *Cannery Row*, startled by the smell of salt air. *A Passage to India*, with its pivotal scenes in the Marabar Caves, is appropriate practically everywhere; ditto *The Plague*, with its rats.

Now, traveling to work from the Bronx, I have plenty of time for books. I am tempted every morning, as I have always been, to stay on the train past my stop, forsaking my job for a ride to the end of the line. Those distant destinations are graced with names that are poetry: Stillwell and Pelham Bay, White Plains Road. The 7 line ends in Flushing at a station called Main Street. Would I find clapboard houses there, and a band shell, and a big statue in the town square of Thornton Wilder? Probably not. Neither do I think it likely that Stillwell is any cheerier a place than Dyre. But then again it doesn't matter. There are always new places to go, and new books to read while going. The journey is the thing. No smoking, spitting, or carrying an open flame, please.

Patrick Flynn, formerly of the Bronx, has relocated to upstate New York. His essays have appeared in The New York Times, The New York Daily News, culturefront, Modern Bride, *and other publications. He is the author of a novel,* Agnes Among the Gargoyles.

SUBWAY MARINER

Stan Fischler

To Coney Island

To me, a kid from Williamsburg, Brooklyn, the idea of taking a trip to Coney Island was roughly equivalent to reading a Buck 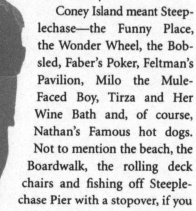 Rogers comic book about his rocket rides to Shangri La—otherworldly.

Coney Island meant Steeplechase—the Funny Place, the Wonder Wheel, the Bobsled, Faber's Poker, Feltman's Pavilion, Milo the Mule-Faced Boy, Tirza and Her Wine Bath and, of course, Nathan's Famous hot dogs. Not to mention the beach, the Boardwalk, the rolling deck chairs and fishing off Steeplechase Pier with a stopover, if you were old enough, for a beer at the Atlantis, where Mousic Powell's dance band played for an eternity.

Coney was Christmas in July (August, too) and getting there was, at the very least, half the fun.

There was only one "best" way to reach the beach, and that was via the West End, Sea Beach, Culver, or Brighton Lines; all of them rolled into the vast Stillwell Avenue Terminal, which also housed a separate trolley station for the Norton's Point streetcar that connected to Sea Gate, an exclusive residential community at the western tip of Coney Island.

Riding each line had its merit, but none could match the surplus of thrills offered by the Brighton run, which boasted two distinctly different sections: one departed from Times Square and the other from Franklin Avenue and Fulton Street in Brooklyn. The best part of the Brighton ride was its rolling stock. If ever there was a Rolls-Royce of subway cars, it was the Brooklyn-Manhattan Transit Company's (BMT) Standard, which was introduced to the Brighton Line during World War I and—with improvements over two decades— was still in service when I began riding in the late 1930s. Five-passenger rattan seats were a feature of its interior, along with three sets of wide, sliding doors and large overhead fans that seemed to spin faster than airplane propellers. The most youngster-friendly item was a tiny rattan jump seat just to the left of the front window. The seat—about two feet by two feet square—was always in the open position and almost never was occupied by a passenger.

Even a four-year-old could hoist himself up and onto the jump seat, which is precisely what I did in 1936 for my world premiere ride on the Brighton Line. Designers of the BMT Standard were considerate enough to provide a front window. The top of the window had a pair of knobs on each side. By grasping and then pressing the knobs with index fingers and thumbs, I could manage to lower the window down each brass ratchet until the opening was wide enough to fit a head, and then some! Having an open front window available enhanced the ride tenfold. Since the jump seat was just across from the motorman's cabin, I could pretend to be the motorman of the eight-car train while at the same time enjoying the rush of wind through my hair as the BMT Standard picked up speed en route to the beach.

The open window also brought me so close to the track itself that I could hear every significant subway sound, from the screech of flange against rail to the special *clickety-clack* of wheels rolling over the rail gaps. Almost sensuous to the ear, the *clickety-clack* replicated contemporary jazz rhythms, including Gene Krupa's drumming behind Benny Goodman's "After You've Gone" or "The World Is Waiting for the Sunrise." The rhythms so intoxicated my youthful brain that I soon figured out how to duplicate them with my lips and tongue so that I could pretend, while walking down the street, that I was a BMT Standard barreling past the Cortelyou Road local station in Flatbush.

Since we lived on Marcy near Myrtle Avenue in Brooklyn, we were nowhere near a Brighton Line station. Two choices were available: the Myrtle Avenue elevated line (a block away) downtown to the Flatbush Avenue extension, or the IND subway (also a block away)—with one change of line—to Franklin Avenue.

The run from Franklin Avenue was preferable on several counts. For starters, this version of the Brighton Express began its journey from an old elevated station at the corner of Franklin and Fulton Streets. During the winter this was the Franklin Avenue Shuttle, which stopped at only a few stations between Fulton Street and Prospect Park. But in the summertime BMT officials had the good sense to allow it to run past Prospect Park and all the way to Coney Island. To distinguish one Franklin version of the Brighton Express from the other, BMT dispatchers affixed a large white disk to the front bumper, which gave the train an even more important look. To me it was like the Orient Express of Brooklyn.

The most exciting aspect of the jaunt from Fulton Street to Prospect Park was the decline from the elevated portion to street level and then down to the tunnel portal at Empire Boulevard. It was at this point that the tracks curved sharply to the right and then just as sharply to the left before reaching the Prospect Park station. Like many other Brooklynites, I knew that this was the precise point where a Brighton Express crashed on the night of November 1, 1918, killing ninety-seven riders. It was known as the Great Malbone Street Wreck and had become synonymous with tragedy throughout the borough. (Family legend had it that a distant relative was on the doomed train and survived, but this never could be verified.) When the crash occurred, the Brooklyn Rapid Transit (BRT), the company that preceded the BMT, was operating fragile, wooden cars that splintered on impact. They lacked the fail-safe "automatic tripper" attached to more modern cars that would have brought the train to a safer halt even though it was traveling an estimated fifty miles per hour in a six-mile-per-hour zone. Just the idea of riding these same tracks through the same tunnel in which the Brighton Express crashed was both fascinating and exhilarating to me. And the idea of the train being able to negotiate the pair of ninety-degree curves was awesome.

Getting to Coney Island involved three contrasting aspects of out-of-doors subwaying all on the Brighton Line—the open cut, the dirt embankment, and the steel elevated portion.

From Prospect Park, the four-track open cut was like a railway canyon, extending from the Prospect Park station, past Parkside Avenue station, followed by the Beverly and Cortelyou Road local stops, concluding at Newkirk Avenue, the last express stop on the open cut portion of the Brighton Line. Each of these stations was graced with bright red, steel chewing gum machines not seen on other lines. The Brighton Line stations offered Pulver Chewing Gum in a dispenser that looked more at home in a Coney Island penny arcade than a subway station. In addition to dispensing three tasty flavors of gum, the crimson Pulver machine had an extra attraction. Behind a glass cover, a pair of "performers" would swing into motion at the drop of a penny into the gum slot. At the moment the machine swallowed its penny, the cop, wielding a nightstick, began banging the robber on top of the head until the stick of gum appeared and sat at the bottom of the red machine.

Continuing south from Newkirk station, the BMT Standard ascended a rather steep hill until it passed the Avenue H station, where it seemed the whole of Flatbush was laid out before you. The embankment, with its straightaway four-track layout, had all the feel of a standard transcontinental railway. The express run from Newkirk to Kings Highway was long, straight, and filled with marvelous sights and sounds. With my head out the window, I could hear every movement of the wheels over the rails because the tracks were sitting on dirt, not concrete or steel. The sound and rhythm was matched in excitement only by the rush of wind on my face as the express virtually leaped past George W. Wingate field on the left and the old Vitagraph Studios movie set on the right. After a brief respite at Kings Highway, the Standard picked up speed at Sheepshead Bay, where the dirt embankment merged with the steel trestle and a different—more raucous—sound was produced as the Atlantic Ocean suddenly dominated the landscape.

The *ch-ch-ch* sound of the air brakes signaled that a ninety-degree curve was ahead. I never felt quite sure that the trains would be able to negotiate the right turn over Coney Island Avenue and into the Brighton Beach station. But this all was part of the transit melodrama. The smell of the briny deep penetrated my nostrils as we headed west over Brighton Beach Avenue toward the concrete art nouveau station straddling Ocean Parkway. It had a massive feel unlike any station on the line.

Then came a puzzle, because the Brighton Line would merge with the Sea Beach, West End, and Culver runs. To accommodate the three units, engineers built a two-tiered elevated structure leading into the Stillwell Avenue terminal. Which elevated track would the Brighton Express take? It was impossible to tell whether it would be routed down to the lower el or—thrill of thrills—climb to the high el with the most splendid panorama of Coney Island attractions along Surf Avenue.

Approaching the Stillwell Terminal, our express had to negotiate one more screeching curve, which heralded our arrival into the land of cotton candy, french fries, and frozen custard. Coney Island, I had arrived!

To the ballparks

As a native Brooklynite, I started my baseball rooting career at Ebbets Field, home of the Brooklyn Dodgers. The ballpark, dating back to 1913, was on Sullivan Place at the very bottom of Crown Heights. It overlooked the Botanic Gardens and Prospect Park to the west and Empire Boulevard (originally Malbone Street), which separated the Flatbush and Crown Heights neighborhoods, to the south.

Three subway lines converged on the Dodgers' home park. One was the (IRT) New Lots Avenue Line operated under Eastern Parkway. To reach the ballpark, I'd occasionally get off at the Franklin Avenue station and walk down the hill along Franklin to the stadium. I rarely used that route because (a) I wasn't an IRT fan, and (b) the walk was longer than the others.

Two BMT lines took me a lot closer to the famed Ebbets rotunda. The Franklin Avenue Shuttle had a stop at Botanic Garden, while the Brighton Line stopped at the Prospect Park express station, which was the one used by most Dodger fans. Each of the BMT stations was a five-minute walk from the ticket wickets. It was a fun walk because of the plentiful sights and smells around Prospect Park station. The moment I reached the top of the stairs, I inhaled the sweet smells emanating from Bond Bread's huge bakery on Flatbush Avenue. Once I crossed to Empire Boulevard, hot-peanut vendors lined the route along with *Brooklyn Eagle* newsboys hawking copies of the newspaper as well as free scorecards for the day's game. Ebbets Field's rotunda swallowed the incoming fans, who purchased their tickets, entered the turnstiles, and then climbed the long, concrete ramps to the grandstands and boxes.

Trips to the Polo Grounds to watch the Giants play were less frequent since I was not a Giants fan and the horseshoe-shaped stadium was not only in another borough but way up in Manhattan's northern tier. That was the bad news. The good news was the subway ride on the Independent Subway System (IND), the first built by the city after the IRT and BMT were privately operated. The trip to the Polo Grounds was special. It included one of the longest and fastest nonstop runs on the entire system, from 59th to 125th Street, under Central Park West in Manhattan, and then another neat sprint from 125th to 145th Street under St. Nicholas Avenue.

I started the Polo Grounds jaunt at my home station, Myrtle–Willoughby on the GG, the Brooklyn-Queens Crosstown Line, and then changed at the vast, six-track Hoyt-Schermerhorn terminal in Downtown Brooklyn. The IND cars operating in the years through World War II were part of the R-1 through R-9 rolling stock. They were supposed to be an upgrade on the BMT Standard and, in some ways, were better, but not from a train buff's viewpoint. While there was a large front window, it lacked the Standard's special feature; it could not be opened, and that was a crusher. On the other hand, the IND's pane of glass was considerably larger than that on its BMT counterpart, which made it easier for more than one person to scout the track ahead.

The best part of the trek began at High Street station in Brooklyn, where the squarish tunnel gave way to the circular tubes that snaked under the East River to Manhattan. This was the first opportunity for the A express to free itself from the twists and turns of Brooklyn and go full tilt underwater. I considered every trip from High Street to Broadway/Nassau Street station in Manhattan a special thrill.

It all had to do with a *Sub-Mariner* comic book I had read in my very early years. One chapter told about an enemy plot to sabotage the East River subway tunnel and—with vivid drawings—depicted the underwater tunnel being pierced by an explosion, whereupon the subway trains were flooded on the riverbed. The question I posed to myself as the A train began its descent under the river was this: Would the tunnel somehow be damaged, and what would happen if the gallons upon gallons of water crashed through the tunnel while my train was destined for Broadway/Nassau? If nothing else, it made for a melodramatic ride!

Once in Manhattan, the A took its time about being a *real* express. There were a couple of short dashes before Columbus Circle, but nothing compared to what would come after 59th Street station. Designers of the original Eighth Avenue (IND) Subway had a two-tiered arrangement of express and local trains running under Central Park West. Uptown trains ran on the upper level while the downtown local and express operated below. This made for most interesting train-watching, since we train buffs were accustomed to four-track operation on one level where express and locals plied the same route rather than a pair of tracks atop the other.

Since IND tracks were laid in concrete—as opposed to dirt and ballast for the IRT and BMT—the decibel count was significantly higher for the A express. As the train passed the 86th and 96th Street stations, it created a thunder all its own which, combined with the speed, made it one of the most arresting experiences for any subway fan. Adding to the kick of it all was the manner in which it changed from a two-tiered to traditional four-track system at 110th Street/Cathedral Parkway, at the northern tip of Central Park. By the time the A train ran through the 116th Street Station, it was time for the motorman to hit the brakes, and we glided into 125th Street, and I sensed that the express was as exhausted by the sixty-six-block race as I was having endured it.

Originally located at 110th Street and Fifth Avenue, the Polo Grounds moved to 155th Street and Eighth Avenue in 1889. Its odd, horseshoe shape was much better suited for football than baseball, but that hardly detracted from its appeal as a stadium. In fact, the geographic oddity of its layout actually lent an intriguing feel to the Polo Grounds, especially since polo never was played at the transplanted, uptown ballpark. Once the scourge of the National League, the Giants had lost considerable prestige by the time I made my first trip to their Harlem home. Still, having been accustomed to tiny Ebbets Field, I was awed by the 55,000-seat Polo Grounds.

The redeeming aspect of an excursion to Yankee Stadium was that it would provide one of the few opportunities to ride what I considered the quaintest of our three subway lines, the IRT. My connecting station was Broadway/Nassau in lower Manhattan, where I changed from the IND A train to the Jerome/Lexington Avenue IRT Express. Like its West Side counterpart, the Lex provided several good runs—such as 14th to 42nd Streets; 42nd to 86th; and 86th to 125th.

The end of the trip to Yankee Stadium was the best part. Just before reaching the elevated 161st Street station, the Express negotiated a long right-handed curve out of the tunnel, passing directly behind the outfield wall. Ever since the stadium was completed in 1923, the elevated line has been part of the woof and warp of the ballpark's landscape.

Everything about the IRT was outlandish to me. Its subway cars were conspicuously thinner than those on the other two lines, and the tunnels had a smaller look. In the late 1930s, when the IRT was still privately operated, its standard car dated back to 1916. The Low-V was idiosyncratic in several ways. Its motors groaned considerably louder than those on the IND or BMT. When a Low-V approached, I had the distinct impression I was standing outside an abattoir. At times, it was almost painful to be assailed by the noise. It had three doors that, unlike other cars, slid from side to side instead of meeting at the middle. A huge hunk of rubber covered the end of the door, making it very easy to hold it open for an approaching passenger. For front window–viewing purposes, the Low-V was a treat because even though the window didn't open, there was a secondary viewing position on the far left side of the train, which meant that at least four train buffs could enjoy the view.

When it came to baseball, Dad and I had our most fun on Sunday afternoons when the Dodgers were on the road and we trained out to one of the most pleasant ballparks in America, Dexter Park, home of the (Brooklyn) Bushwicks. It was located shoulder to shoulder with Franklin K. Lane High School on the Brooklyn–Queens border. The Cypress Hills neighborhood was on the Brooklyn side, and Woodhaven was on the Queens side. I believe the county line ran directly through home plate, second base, and centerfield.

Of all the stadia in New York City, the mass transit trip to Dexter Park was the most scenic. From Williamsburg to Cypress Hills/ Woodhaven, the entire trip was aboveground and on some of the most unique track beds. The elevated line was the best way to get to Dexter Park. Dad and I would walk a half-block to Myrtle Avenue and then a full block underneath the Myrtle Avenue El to Tompkins Avenue. One of the oldest elevated lines in New York, the Myrtle route had a charm all its own. Rolling stock dated back to the nineteenth century. Cars had open platforms at each end with conductors manning steel gates between each car. When the last car's conductor was ready to flash his "all-clear" signal, he pulled on a cord that rang a bell for the conductor straddling the cars ahead of him. This was repeated until the bell rang in the motorman's compartment and another run began.

No less unique were the stations themselves. We had to climb two sets of staircases to reach the cashier's booth. Like a miniature waiting room on a rural railway, the Myrtle station featured everything from pot-bellied stoves to ancient turnstiles with thick pieces of copper that jangled sweetly as they turned.

Outdoor platforms were made of wood with steel beams holding up the roof. When trains approached, the entire station seemed to tremble, leading me to wonder if the whole shebang would simply collapse onto the street below. Myrtle's el had a distinct rhythm to it, which was a function of the rail gaps and the train speed, which fluctuated between languid and lethargic. Since stations were usually spaced only two blocks apart, it would have been difficult to pick up much speed. The percussive rail sounds almost could be equated with a waltz tempo, *ta-ta-ta . . . ta-ta-ta,* which increased in tempo as the ancient cars accelerated toward the next station. But after one block's worth of momentum, the motorman was compelled to shut down his controller and begin braking to a stop.

Like the BMT Standard, Myrtle's unique cars had several added attractions for train buffs like me. The open platform between cars was a treat because it allowed a passenger to stand outside and watch the passing parade on the street below, not to mention fascinating sights through the windows of second-story apartment buildings.

During the summer, which was when we went to see the Bushwicks, the BMT operated cars with open sides that allowed cool breezes to flow through the cars. Although the window on the front car did not open, the door did. That meant that I could actually stand by the door opening—the platform was still ahead—and look out at the tracks before me without any encumbrances whatsoever. The fact that the Myrtle line didn't go very fast hardly mattered; in fact, the slow speed was a virtue in this case because there was so much to see.

Our ride on the el to Dexter Park took only a few minutes because we got off at Broadway (Brooklyn) Junction, a major intersection of two lines. The Myrtle el continued east to Metropolitan Avenue, while the BMT Broadway Line had crossed the Williamsburg Bridge and was proceeding to its terminus in Jamaica, Queens.

Built in 1908, the Broadway el began its run in Manhattan's financial district, then rolled past Williamsburg and Bushwick in Brooklyn en route to a monstrous meeting of the rails at Eastern Parkway/East New York Junction. When the el reached Crescent Street station, it was staring ahead to Fulton Street, although the tracks curved sharply to the left toward Cypress Hills. I always found myself fixing a glance at the distinguished-looking Hamburg Savings Bank Building at the intersection of Crescent and Fulton Streets. As the train screeched around the ninety-degree turn, it passed over the building. I figured that if the motorman ever allowed his consist to get out of control, the train would plunge right on top of the bank roof. It made for an exciting turn.

Three blocks to the north, the Broadway el executed another ninety-degree turn, this time to the right over the Jamaica Avenue and Cypress Hills stations. To the right was a large, private club with a gigantic pool and a lengthy slide that deposited swimmers into the water. I longed to go down that slide but was assured by my father that we would not be welcomed in Cypress Hills.

Our train ride to Dexter Park ended at Elderts Lane station. I fairly well danced down the steps in anticipation of getting to watch the Bushwicks play ball. We crossed Jamaica Avenue under the el, along a dirt path to the wooden ticket windows where Dad plunked down his three quarters. A news hawk sold us a program and we proceeded to the third-base grandstand, although the ballpark had open bleachers past third and first base. There also were a handful of bleacher seats in left and center fields, but we always sat in the third-base grandstand.

My dad and I had a post–double-header ritual at the Automat, a popular cafeteria run by an outfit called Horn and Hardart. Instead of going straight home after a double-header, we would board the Broadway Line and take it back to Myrtle Avenue, where we'd transfer to the Myrtle el heading to Downtown Brooklyn. I'd stand at the back end of the platform and peer eastward down the tracks until the open-ended trains hovered into view. Dad and I would remain on the local all the way to Fulton Street. This meant I had the luxury of standing by the open front door as the train moved through Williamsburg, Clinton Hill, and the Navy Yard district before crossing the long, steel Flatbush Avenue Extension trestle that signaled we were downtown and near the Automat, where I could get a full-bodied and rich hot chocolate for a nickel. It was the perfect end to a perfect el-riding day.

Former Mayor Rudolf Giuliani named **Stan Fischler** *one of a select group of One Hundred Distinguished New York Historians, in honor of Fischler's work as the most prolific subway historian. His first such book,* Uptown, Downtown: A Trip Through Time on New York's Subways, *was highly acclaimed by critics and remains the most celebrated book on the subject. Since then, Fischler has written several landmark books on subways including* Moving Millions, *a definitive history of transit worldwide, and* Subways of the World. *His most recent book,* The Subway and the City *was designated by the Metropolitan Transit Authority as an official Centennial volume honoring the New York underground's hundredth birthday in 2004.*

A SIGNIFICANT
COINCIDENCE

Tim Steffen

With one breath, with one flow, you will know . . . synchronicity.
—The Police

I grew up with music. My three older sisters played piano. Our youngest sister, Kathy, could play any instrument. Truly. She could pick up and play a guitar, flute, banjo—you name it. She was always on the *que vive* for something new to play. We hated her for it. Show-off.

Before I turned six there was talk in the house that I was soon to begin lessons. I looked forward to it, but when my instruction with Mrs. Durand began, I was fully frustrated. I wanted to play right away. I immediately wanted my fingers to do what my mom's and sisters' did, but the first year of lessons was a persecution upon me and those within earshot. I couldn't play worth a tinker's cuss; not one jot, not one tittle.

I was home during my freshman winter break from college, playing the piano in our living room, when Mom asked me, "Do you remember that bit of psychology I used to use with you?" I didn't, but then, as she told me,

197

I became that six-year-old boy again, the one with the bangs and cowlick, sitting on that same piano bench. In the first year I knew how bad I sounded and banged on the piano quite often. Just when I was about to give up, Mom would always chime in lightly from the kitchen: "That sounded great, Timmy. You're getting better." *Really? I guess I should keep practicing.*

Whenever I expressed my frustration verbally, threatening to quit, Mom would tell me how she felt the same way about the piano when she was learning, but was always sure to add, "It'll give you joy throughout your life."

I kept banging, Mom kept complimenting no matter what, and one day it clicked. I understood the piano, the music. It all made sense. The monkey ate his banana.

Music continues to energize my life. I get ample doses of it underground, from the ubiquitous Peruvian pan flute players to Robert Johnson–inspired blues guitar to that odd-spectacled woman who plays the Theremin-sounding saw.

One night, coming back from a March birthday party on the Upper West Side, I hopped the downtown 1 with friends Don and Mel then transferred at 42nd Street. As we walked downstairs to the N/R line, we heard the music of a violin and followed it until we were at the middle of the platform. A man played an Irish reel. St. Patty's Day was only a few days away.

He smiled as if he knew us, and immediately after he finished his song he glided over and extended the violin and bow toward Don, nodding his head.

"Play something," the man said.

Don laughed and said he didn't play. Mel echoed the same response as the man once again offered the instrument.

"You?" he asked me, an Indian accent coming through a wide smile set on a russet face.

When I was thirteen and wanted a new instrument to bang on, I had asked my parents if I could take violin lessons. Lessons cost money. By then, my two oldest sisters were in college and one was planning on getting married. My dad was working overtime at Mobil Oil and painting houses on weekends. Mom had returned to work as a part-time secretary at Mobil. My parents looked at each other with raised brows. Dad shrugged his shoulders and Mom's eyes twinkled. I knew the answer before they said it. My dad even knew a guy at work who played violin in the community orchestra. "I'll ask him tomorrow."

Mr. Wuertz agreed to teach me and charged us basically nothing for a lesson. I think it was ten dollars. He worked with me for three years until he died of throat cancer. I didn't want to take lessons with anyone else. I had also stopped piano lessons at that time. I was sixteen; I knew I didn't want a career in music.

My violin now rests in the uppermost regions of my closet. Occasionally, when I need something else up there I dust off the case and open the tarnished lock. The hinges simultaneously creak. The violin coughs as I pick it up. I tighten the horsehair bow and play a few measures of "Eine Kleine Nachtmusik" before putting it back to bed until next time.

"You?" the man on the platform asked again.

I told him that yes, I played, but not very well. Truly. I'm not really that good, a few squeaks here and there, but I get by.

"Please, play," he said with more enthusiasm. "Something Irish. I cannot read music. I need to hear and I learn. Please, play."

At first I couldn't think of any Irish tunes, and then I remembered something I believe is called "Irish Washerwoman." The man smiled while I played, watching my fingers move up and down the strings, studying each note, writing them down in his mind.

I looked around the best I could while I played the song and noticed several people watching the curiosity unfold. I don't know any other word to describe the looks on their faces except bemused, as if they too would never expect someone to hand them a violin, but wouldn't necessarily mind.

I finished the little ditty and returned his violin. The man thanked me. I told him how well he played. He shook his head and put up a hand. "No, no, I'm not that good," he said, "but I believe in reincarnation and that I will play at Carnegie Hall in the next life. Right now, in this lifetime, I'm just practicing."

There was some kind of wonderful energy on that platform. No coincidence. Perhaps it was what Jung calls a "significant coincidence," the signs in which two people have detected a phenomenon of synchrony that reveals an unsuspected connection between man, time, and space. I believe that somehow, unconsciously or consciously, the man was aware that one in our group of three knew how to play the violin.

The train pulled up and the moment passed.

Being aware of moments like this one is my life's practice. They connect me to something larger yet are still a part of me. I feel less lonely. Riding the subway allows me the moments to connect with people, something I rarely get to do when I'm biking around the city, my mind on the destination and what I'm going to do when I get there. A friend likes to tell me that I have to throw the monkey a banana sometimes. The subway is my busy mind's banana.

I'm only limited by my imagination.

One year and six days later, I was going home after a very long day of teaching and grad school. A little music would have been nice, but I had forgotten my iPod. I walked quickly down Broadway around 110th Street, and I could hear the downtown train approaching underneath my feet. My focus was getting on that train. I ran down two steps at a time, gripping the railing, quickly thinking of all the germs that I was picking up on my hand because I had forgotten my gloves that morning.

I swiped my Metrocard, lunged through the turnstile as the train pulled up and stopped. I heard a violin, looked to my right as I stepped on the train, saw the Indian violinist, and realized he was playing the same song I had taught him a year ago.

I looked out the train window as my car passed him and I was gone. I stared at the lights on the subway walls passing by the window in rapid succession to form a continuous stream of light. It felt so very sci-fi to be on a train underground, traveling hypnotically under the feet of a million souls. I threw the monkey a banana, my mind slowed down, and I was totally in the moment with no future or past, just being on the train between stations as "Irish Washerwoman" sang in my head along with Mom's voice: "It'll give you joy throughout your life."

Tim Steffen *is a writer, illustrator, spoonerist, and early childhood teacher at a private school in Manhattan. He plays ragtime piano on Fire Island in the summers and is an occasional violinist. His work can be viewed at www.timsteffen.com.*

CONTRIBUTORS

Jacquelin Cangro founded thesubwaychronicles.com in 2002. The site quickly gained popularity and became the inspiration for this anthology. Jacquelin has published short stories in literary magazines including *The MacGuffin* and *Pangolin Papers*; she is currently writing her first novel.

A cultural essayist specializing in tales of personal adventure, **Anastasia M. Ashman** co-edited *Tales from the Expat Harem: Foreign Women in Modern Turkey* (Seal Press 2006). She has appeared in publications worldwide, from the *Asian Wall Street Journal* to the *Village Voice*. Currently living in Istanbul with her Turkish husband, she is at work on a travel memoir, *Berkeley to Byzantium: The Reorientation of a West Coast Adventuress*. When in New York, she's loyal to the N and the R.

Lawrence Block's novels range from the urban noir of Matthew Scudder (*All the Flowers Are Dying*) to the urbane effervescence of Bernie Rhodenbarr (*The Burglar on the Prowl*), while other characters include the globe-trotting insomniac Evan Tanner (*Tanner on Ice*) and the introspective assassin Keller (*Hit List*).

He has published articles and short fiction in *American Heritage, Redbook, Playboy, Cosmopolitan, GQ,* and *The New York Times,* and eighty-four of his short stories have been collected in *Enough Rope.* His newest bestsellers are *All the Flowers Are Dying* (February 2005 in hardcover), the sixteenth Matthew Scudder novel, and *The Burglar on the Prowl,* his tenth Bernie Rhodenbarr novel now available in paperback. Larry is a Grand Master of Mystery Writers of America and a past president of both MWA and the Private Eye Writers of America. He has won the Edgar and Shamus Awards four times each and the Japanese Maltese Falcon Award twice, as well as the Nero Wolfe and Philip Marlowe awards, a Lifetime Achievement Award from the Private Eye Writers of America and, most recently, the Cartier Diamond Dagger for Life Achievement from the Crime Writers Association (UK). Larry and his wife, Lynne, are enthusiastic New Yorkers and relentless world travelers.

Garrett Chaffin-Quiray was educated at the University of Southern California School of Cinema-Television and has sponsored film festivals, taught writing and media history, and published work in various newspapers, magazines, books, and online journals. He now lives in, and writes from, San Diego County.

David Ebershoff is the author of two novels, *The Danish Girl* and *Pasadena.* He is an editor-at-large at Random House, and is finishing a new novel, *The 19th Wife.* He can be reached at www.ebershoff.com.

Former Mayor Rudolf Giuliani named **Stan Fischler** one of a select group of One Hundred Distinguished New York Historians, in honor of Fischler's work as the most prolific subway historian. His first such book, *Uptown, Downtown: A Trip Through Time on New York's Subways,* was highly acclaimed by critics and remains the most celebrated book on the subject. Since then, Fischler has written several landmark books on subways including *Moving Millions,* a definitive history of transit worldwide, and *Subways of* *the World.* His most recent book, *The Subway and the City* was designated by the Metropolitan Transit Authority as an official Centennial volume honoring the New York underground's hundredth birthday in 2004.

Boris Fishman is the editor of *Wild East: Stories from the Last Frontier.* He has written for *The New Yorker, The New York Times Magazine, The New Republic, The Nation,* and other publications.

Patrick Flynn, formerly of the Bronx, has relocated to upstate New York. His essays have appeared in *The New York Times, The New York Daily News, culturefront, Modern Bride,* and other publications. He is the author of a novel, *Agnes Among the Gargoyles.*

Vivian Gornick writes memoirs, essays, and literary criticism. Among her books are *Fierce Attachments, The End of the Novel of Love,* and *The Situation and the Story.* Her newest book is a biographical essay: *The Solitude of Self: Thinking About Elizabeth Cady Stanton.* She lives in New York City.

Amy Holman is the author of *An Insider's Guide to Creative Writing Programs,* published with Perigee in 2006, and the poetry collection, *Wait For Me, I'm Gone,* published with Dream Horse Press. She teaches writers how to get published at The New School University, Spalding University, Hudson Valley Writers Center, Bread Loaf Writers Conference, and others. She is a poet and prose writer living near the F Line in Brooklyn, New York, and her writing been published in *The Best American Poetry 1999, The History of Panty Hose in America, AWP JobLetter, Poets & Writers* magazine, and many print and online literary journals.

Elise Juska grew up outside Philadelphia and received her master's in fiction writing from the University of New Hampshire in 1997, where she won the graduate writing awards for best short story and overall body of fiction. Her short stories have since appeared in several magazines, including the *Harvard Review, Salmagundi, Seattle Review, Black Warrior Review*, and *The Hudson Review*. She teaches fiction workshops at the University of the Arts in Philadelphia and the New School in New York City. Currently she is working on her third novel, forthcoming from Simon & Schuster in 2007.

Jessie Koester is the director of Information Services at *Poets & Writers*. She has an MFA from The New School and recently received a fellowship from Yaddo, where she worked toward completing her first novel.

Robert Lanham is the author of the beach-towel classic *The Emerald Beach Trilogy* which includes the titles *Pre-Coitus, Coitus*, and *Aftermath*. More recent works include *Food Court Druids, Cherohonkees and Other Creatures Unique to the Republic*, and *The Hipster Handbook*. Lanham's writing has appeared in *The New York Times, Nylon, The Washington Post, Playboy*, and *Time Out*. He is currently working on a new book about Evangelical Christianity in America. He is the editor and founder of www.freewilliamsburg .com and lives in Brooklyn, New York.

Jonathan Lethem is the author of six novels, including *The Fortress of Solitude* and *Motherless Brooklyn*, which won the National Book Critics Circle Award. He is also the author of two short-story collections, *Men and Cartoons* and *The Wall of the Sky, the Wall of the Eye*, and is the editor of *The Vintage Book of Amnesia*. His essays have appeared in *The New Yorker, Rolling Stone, Granta*, and *Harper's*. He was the recipient of a MacArthur Fellowship in 2005. He lives in Brooklyn and Maine.

Megan Lyles grew up in Brooklyn near the Fort Hamilton Parkway stop on the B line. She has fond memories of the time when trains were decorated with graffiti and cooled naturally by open windows. Now a travel writer based in Manhattan, she still sometimes stands at the door in the very front of the train to watch the tunnel rush at her, but she manages to resist the temptation to swing around the poles. Visit her Web site at www.meganlyles.com.

Tim McLoughlin's debut novel, *Heart of the Old Country*, was a selection of the Barnes & Noble Discover Great New Writers program and has been optioned for a film. He is the editor of the *Brooklyn Noir* anthology series, and his short fiction has been included in the *Best American Mystery Stories 2005*.

Daniels Parseliti is a writer living in Queens, New York. He spends his time making fiction, philosophy, and pasta sauce, though only the sauce yields income. He has co-written a play that was produced twice in NYC and is currently working on a novel. Daniels can be reached at intuitconcept@hotmail.com.

Francine Prose's most recent books are *A Changed Man*, a novel, and *Caravaggio: Painter of Miracles*, which is part of the Eminent Lives series. Her novel *Blue Angel*, was a finalist for the National Book Award. *Reading Like a Writer*, a book about learning to write by reading literature, will appear from HarperCollins in fall 2006. She is a contributing editor at *Harper's* and writes frequently for numerous other publications.

April Reynolds has taught at New York University and is currently teaching creative writing at Sarah Lawrence College. Her short stories have appeared in several anthologies. Published by Metropolitan Books/Henry Holt in 2003, her first novel, *Knee-Deep in Wonder* won the Zora Neale Hurston/Richard Wright Foundation Award and the PEN American Center: Beyond Margins Award. Her second book is forthcoming from Free Press/Simon & Schuster.

Lucinda Rosenfeld is the author of the novels *What She Saw . . .* and *Why She Went Home*. Her fiction and essays have appeared in the *New Yorker*, the *Sunday Telegraph*, *New York Magazine*, and *Glamour*.

Tim Steffen is a writer, illustrator, spoonerist, and early childhood teacher at a private school in Manhattan. He plays ragtime piano on Fire Island in the summers and is an occasional violinist. His work can be viewed at www.timsteffen.com.

Leigh Stolle worked as a journalist before earning an MFA in creative writing from Emerson College. She currently lives on the Upper East Side of Manhattan and is working on a collection of short stories.

Johnny Temple is the publisher and editor-in-chief of Akashic Books, an award-winning New York–based independent company dedicated to publishing urban literary fiction and political nonfiction. He won the American Association of Publishers 2005 Miriam Bass Award for Creativity in Independent Publishing. Temple plays bass guitar in two bands, Girls Against Boys and New Wet Kojak; both bands have toured extensively across the globe and released numerous albums. Temple has contributed articles and political essays to various publications, including *The Nation*, *Publishers Weekly*, *AlterNet*, *Alternative Press*, *Poets & Writers*, and *Bust*.

Jennifer Toth is the author of *The Mole People: Life in the Tunnels Beneath New York City* (Chicago Review Press, 1993), *Orphans of the Living: Stories of America's Children in Foster Care* (Simon & Schuster, 1997), and *What Happened to Johnnie Jordan? The Story of A Child Turning Violent* (The Free Press, 2002). She is currently living in Berlin with her husband, Craig Whitlock—a reporter for *The Washington Post*—and her son, Kyle.

Calvin Trillin has been writing for *The New Yorker* for more than thirty years. His many books include *Tepper Isn't Going Out, Travels with Alice, Remembering Denny, Family Man, The Tummy Trilogy, Deadline Poet,* and *Too Soon to Tell.*

Ken Wheaton was born and raised in Opelousas, Louisiana. There, he drove a 1985 Honda CRX. He now calls Brooklyn his home and the 4 train his ride. He writes for *Advertising Age* magazine, dabbles in fiction and wastes hours blogging at http://nondatinglife.blogspot.com.

Colson Whitehead was born and raised in New York City. He is the author of *The Intuitionist* and *John Henry Days* and is a recipient of a Whiting Award and a MacArthur Fellowship. He lives in Brooklyn.

Yona Zeldis McDonough is the editor of the essay collections *The Barbie Chronicles: A Living Doll Turns Forty* and *All the Available Light: A Marilyn Monroe Reader* and the author of the novels *The Four Temperaments* and *In Dahlia's Wake.*

ACKNOWLEDGMENTS

Thank you to all of the writers who sent their submissions to the Web site on faith and patiently waited for a response. They are the cornerstones on which this book is founded.

With special thanks to Rick Broadhead, who saw the potential for this project; Meg Leder, a more enthusiastic champion for this book could never be found; and Molly Barton, my dedicated, trustworthy editor with a sharp eye.

I owe tremendous gratitude to these special people: Robin Kaye Llewellyn, Web site designer extraordinaire and wonderful friend; Dawn Techow, for planting the germ of an idea to find a place to gather these stories; Michele Truty, my tireless second set of eyes; Jason Primm, who offered hours of valuable consult free of charge; Catharine Lynch, supporter of the book from the beginning; Jason Warzcheka, who answered my many technical Web site questions with clarity and patience; Maile Chaffin-Quiray, a beacon with a steady beam; Ginny Anson; Doug Whiteman; and especially my mother, to whom I owe eternal gratitude.

Photographs throughout the book:
Details from *Carrying On*, 2004,
© Janet Zweig and Edward del Rosario,
a 1,200' frieze of steel, stone, and tile,
embedded in the walls of the
Prince Street subway station at
Prince and Broadway, New York City.
Commissioned and owned by the
Metropolitan Transportation Authority
Arts for Transit.
Photographs © Cathy Carver.

Pages 211–212 constitute an extension of the copyright page.

Introduction by Jacquelin Cangro. Copyright © 2006 by Jacquelin Cangro. All rights reserved.

"Opening Day" by Tim McLoughlin. Copyright © 2006 by Tim McLoughlin. All rights reserved.

"A Breakup Story" by Francine Prose. Copyright © 2006 by Francine Prose. All rights reserved.

"Porno Man and I Versus the Feminist Avenger and Displaced Anger Man" by Daniels Parseliti. Copyright © 2006 by Daniels Parseliti. All rights reserved.

"Subway" by Colson Whitehead. Copyright © 2003 as part of *The Colossus of New York* by Colson Whitehead. All rights reserved.

"Straphanger Doppelgänger" by Robert Lanham. Copyright © 2006 by Robert Lanham. All rights reserved.

"Transfer" by Leigh Stolle. Copyright © 2006 by Leigh Stolle. All rights reserved.

"Under the Skin" by Yona Zeldis McDonough. Copyright © 2006 by Yona Zeldis McDonough. All rights reserved.

"Bombs! Anthrax! Gas! Ho, Hum." by Ken Wheaton. Copyright © 2006 by Ken Wheaton. All rights reserved.

"Standing Up" by Megan Lyles. Copyright © 2006 by Megan Lyles. All rights reserved.

"Collecting Old Subway Cars" by Lawrence Block. Copyright © 2006 by Lawrence Block. All rights reserved.

"The First Annual Three-Borough Subway Party" by Johnny Temple. Copyright © 2006 by Johnny Temple. All rights reserved.

"Encounter" by Jessie Koester. Copyright © 2006 by Jessie Koester. All rights reserved.

"Tunnel Stories" by Jennifer Toth. Copyright © 2006 by Jennifer Toth. All rights reserved.

"Speak, Hoyt-Schermerhorn" by Jonathan Lethem. Copyright © 2005 as part of *The Disappointment Artist* by Jonathan Lethem. All rights reserved.

"A Beautiful Boy" by Vivian Gornick. Copyright © 2006 by Vivian Gornick. All rights reserved.

"What's the Good Word?" by Calvin Trillin. Copyright © 1995 by Calvin Trillin. All rights reserved.

"What I Feared" by Elise Juska. Copyright © 2006 by Elise Juska. All rights reserved.

"Lunch Time" by David Ebershoff. Copyright © 2006 by David Ebershoff. All rights reserved.

"Metro Blues, or How I Came to America" by Boris Fishman. Copyright © 2006 by Boris Fishman. All rights reserved.

"An Egg Salad Sandwich on the Red Line" by Anastasia M. Ashman. Copyright © 2006 by Anastasia Ashman. All rights reserved.

"Cups" by Amy Holman Copyright © 2006 by Amy Holman. All rights reserved.

"Is This the Good Samaritan Story?" by April Reynolds. Copyright © 2006 by April Reynolds. All rights reserved.

"Service Advisory" by Garrett Chaffin-Quiray. Copyright © 2006 by Garrett Chaffin-Quiray. All rights reserved.

"If I Were in Charge of the MTA" by Lucinda Rosenfeld. Copyright © 2006 by Lucinda Rosenfeld. All rights reserved.

"Parnassus Underground" by Patrick Flynn. Copyright © 2006 by Patrick Flynn. All rights reserved.

"Subway Mariner" by Stan Fischler. Copyright © 2006 by Stan Fischler. All rights reserved.

"A Significant Coincidence" by Tim Steffen. Copyright © 2006 by Tim Steffen. All rights reserved.